DIVINE SPEARS

KEN CONBOY

DIVINE SPEARS
Operations of Indonesia's Special Forces in East Timor, 1975-77

Equinox Publishing (Asia) Pte. Ltd.
18/F Cyber 2 Tower
Jl. HR Rasuna Said Kav C-25
Jakarta, Indonesia

www.EquinoxPublishing.com

Divine Spears:
Operations of Indonesia's Special Forces in East Timor, 1975-77

ISBN 978-602-70255-5-4

First Equinox Edition 2018

1 3 5 7 9 10 8 6 4 2

Text ©2018 Ken Conboy. All rights reserved.

CONTENTS

Introduction 5

Preface: 3 February 1976 1900 Hours 9

1. Gateway to Hell 13

2. SEROJA 21

3. Pitbull in Pinstripes 31

4. Making the Cut 41

5. RECON 51

6. Hell in a Very, Very Small Place 69

7. Lactos Intolerant 80

8. Thunderclap 89

9. Ramahana 105

10. The Dirty Dozen 115

Index 129

INTRODUCTION

Indonesia has endured more than its share of armed conflicts. None, perhaps, tested its military's mettle more than the two-decade campaign in what is now Timor Leste. What was initially a conventional operation—replete with largescale parachute jumps, naval gunfire support, and amphibious landings—soon devolved into a protracted counter-insurgency effort for control of that territory.

This volume focuses on the initial phase of the East Timor operation, at a period when the Timorese opposition was especially well-armed, disciplined, and exceedingly tenacious. Specifically, it follows the deployment of two teams from the Indonesian Special Forces. These teams were codenamed *nanggala*, the Sanskrit term for a divine spear of Hindu legend. One of the *nanggala* discussed in these pages was handed a conventional mission, the other with a decidedly unconventional orientation. It delves into their successes and shortfalls, and their lessons learned—but not necessarily adopted in the strategy being forged at the time. It is my hope that such a study will be of interest to students of the Indonesian military, conflict in Southeast Asia, and the history of Timor Leste.

This book is possible thanks to the assistance of numerous persons who gave of their time and made available their personal photographs and documents. Among them (in alphabetical order): General (retired) A.M. Hendropriyono, Atmadji Sumarkidjo, Erik Jensen, Fernando Osorio Soares, Francisco Osorio Soares, Major General (retired) Muchdi Purwoprandjono, General (retired) Subagyo H.S., Air Marshal (retired) Subagyo Saleh, Suwito H.A., Vidal Sarmento, and Yudi Karim. Thanks to Andy Setiawan for preparing the maps.

As always, my thanks goes to Mark Hanusz for his yeoman's efforts in editing and producing this volume.

Although all books are a collaborative effort, the author takes responsibility for everything in these pages. Any errors in fact or interpretation are my own.

Ken Conboy
Jakarta, November 2017

PREFACE
3 FEBRUARY 1976 1900 HOURS

Cut into the chalky soil on the southwestern corner of Timor island, Penfui airbase screamed Third World. Aside from a single runway, a rudimentary control tower, and a bunker-like administrative shed, it boasted little else. Even its name—"Corn Forest," from the local dialect—was suitably rustic.

But names can be deceptive. For the duration of World War Two, in fact, Penfui had punched well above its weight. This began in the days immediately after the December 1941 Japanese attack on Pearl Harbor, when Australian military forces rushed to Penfui to reinforce the Dutch and Portuguese garrisons on the island. Albeit briefly, it became a key air-bridge between Darwin and General Douglas MacArthur's forces in the Philippines. Not surprisingly, this attracted Japan's tender mercies, who promptly began pummeling the runway with bombers.[1]

A little over a month later, the script flipped. The Australians abandoned Penfui, and in their wake the Japanese military moved in to make it the southernmost airbase in their Southeast Asian sphere of influence. As this put them within reach of Australia, Penfui became the staging ground for Japanese bombing runs against Darwin—which in turn led Allied aircraft to ravage the runway over the next two years.

Finally, during September 1945 in the wake of Japanese capitulation, Australian forces once more moved back into Penfui to reassert Allied control. By then Penfui's most notable feature was the detritus of war that framed the airfield.

---

[1] Long before an airbase was constructed on the site, Penfui had a bloody backstory. In 1749, a rebellious Timorese army made a stand against the Dutch at Penfui. The Dutch slaughtered thousands in the ensuing fight and emerged victorious, thereby consolidating their colonial grip over the western half of the island.

With this martial background, it was only fitting that on a sweltering night in February 1976, Penfui would again play a key role in the latest military campaign involving Timor. This time Indonesian commandos, nearly 250 in all, were assembled around what was once a hanger aside the runway. The roof had long fallen away, leaving only a rusting frame. Though the sun had set, the lingering humidity and hordes of mosquitos left the soldiers damp and uncomfortable.

An army colonel took to a makeshift podium and in a strained voice began what would pass as a pre-mission briefing. In a few more hours, he announced to the commandos, they would board planes and fly 200 kilometers to the northeast as the crow flies. There they would parachute at dawn to seize the district capital of Suai.

Their target came as no surprise, as they had gotten a mission outline prior to arrival at Penfui. Of concern to them, however, was the fact that there had been no dress rehearsal or even a detailed coordination session. Indeed, half of the commandos had arrived only late that afternoon from Jakarta and the other half from Magelang.

Of equal concern, the briefing failed to include even the most basic information about weather or terrain. Photocopies of a dated Portuguese map were distributed among the task force, but these were in 1:250,000 scale and of little military utility. "It showed the beach, Suai town, and a runway to the northeast," lamented one sergeant. "It didn't have any rivers, or roads, or terrain features."

What the map did show was that Suai was a coastal town, making its proximity to the Timor Sea, and the fact that the jump was at dawn, cause for even further concern: the Indonesian army had conducted a pair of dawn jumps into Timor coastal towns two months prior, and both resulted in fatalities when heavily-laden commandos landed in the water and were instantly swallowed up in the waves.

The colonel continued his briefing. They did not have any firm information about armed Timorese opposition, but they should assume the entire Suai population was hostile. Perhaps remembering that pre-mission briefings for the earlier parachute jumps had been overly optimistic, the colonel made no attempt to sugar-coat his estimate this time around.

"You can expect 50 percent casualties."

A hush fell over the task force as the odds sank in.

"Half of you won't make it."

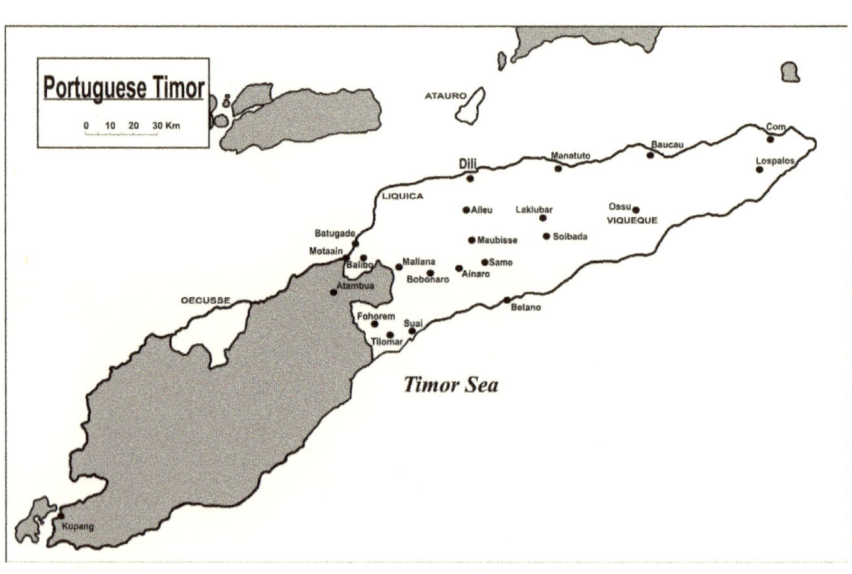

CHAPTER ONE
GATEWAY TO HELL

Events leading up to the parachute jump at Suai were set in motion twenty-two months earlier on the streets of Lisbon. There, a quasi-fascist regime had been firmly in control of Portugal for just over four decades. Like most dictatorships, there was little about it to like. After all, they were not inclined to respect individual liberties at home. And ignoring the wave of post-War de-colonialization, Lisbon refused to cede any of their considerable overseas empire. Worse, after multiple liberation movements sprung up in their African territories in the 1960s, the government saw fit to dedicate a staggering 40 percent of the state budget to maintain a smothering grip over their colonies.

Together, these factors made Portugal increasingly unpopular on the international stage. But within Portugal itself, there was surprisingly little civil resistance. This was probably because the Portuguese economy, despite the heavy burden of funding its colonial wars, still showed promise. And while they bore the brunt of the African conflicts, there was almost no discernible opposition to the dictatorship from the Portuguese military. In fact, with gains being registered in their counter-insurgency campaigns, morale among Portuguese troops was up.

All of this abruptly changed in 1973, when a cabal of young army officers began to plot against the fascists. This was not due to any sense of altruism or idealism. Rather, a dispute had flared over a government plan to quickly boost the number of army officers (for use in Africa) by incorporating militia leaders as equal in rank to military academy graduates. This the regular army could not abide, leading numerous young officers—most of whom were left-leaning—to begin conspiring in plain sight.

What came next could not have been predicted. Rather than cracking down on the wayward officers, the heretofore iron-fisted Portuguese regime showed little appetite to rein in the renegades, who by the opening of 1974 were going by the name Armed Forces Movement (*Movimento das Forças Armadas*, or MFA). In March 1974, the MFA made one unsuccessful attempt to seize power. When the regime offered only a limp response, they tried again on 25 April—this time joined on the streets by a jubilant public that took to placing red carnations in their rifle barrels. The dictatorship summarily wilted, allowing the so-called Carnation Revolution to carry the day against virtually no resistance.

Now in control of the country, the MFA-led junta announced it would steer Portugal along a path toward democracy. They also announced their intent to forfeit the African colonial wars. Making good on this latter promise, by year's end they had withdrawn from Portuguese Guinea. Similarly, they sped up independence preparations for their other African territories.

In Asia, the MFA's attitude toward de-colonization was less consistent. They showed no inclination to part with their tiny but lucrative gambling hub in Macao. In Portuguese Timor, by contrast, all indications pointed toward a velvet divorce from this most distant of possessions. Timor, it seemed, would soon be set free.

*

As backwaters go, Portuguese Timor set the gold standard for underdevelopment. Consisting of just over 15,000 square kilometers spread over half an island (the other half, West Timor, was controlled by Indonesia), one enclave, and a scattering of nearby islets, it was at the farthest end of Lisbon's logistical tether. Not surprisingly, hardly anything reached there even after 500 years of Portugal's so-called civilizing mission. Through World War Two, in fact, Lisbon barely invested in what they less-than-affectionately nicknamed *Ante-câmara do Inferno*—"Gateway to Hell"—because of Timor's omnipresent malaria and other tropical diseases. Such was their level of disinterest, no senior Portuguese cabinet member had ever bothered to set foot in the territory.[1] Rather, they were predisposed to exile their political prisoners to Timor, so much so that political *deportados* outnumbered Portuguese administrators and settlers by the early Twentieth Century.

---

1   Jose Ramos-Horta, Funu, *The Unfinished Saga of East Timor* (Trenton, N.J., The Red Sea Press: 1987), p. 22.

Not until the 1960s did Lisbon give much thought to redressing their benign neglect. Even so, by the time of the MFA coup, Portuguese Timor could still be best described by superlatives—none of them flattering. In the field of education, for example, illiteracy stood at about 93 percent. There was little secondary and no tertiary education. The handful of Timorese that got a university education—there were only a half dozen graduates as of 1974—had to go to Lisbon.²

In terms of infrastructure, electricity did not reach the Timorese capital of Dili until 1970. The rest of the colony relied on firewood and candles. There were no paved roads outside of Dili, though to be fair the gravel roads crisscrossing the territory were adequate in the dry season.

It was in this state of chronic under-development, and with Lisbon telegraphing its intention to leave, that three main Timorese political parties sprang up in 1974. The first to formally take shape was the Timorese Democratic Union (*União Democrática Timorense,* or UDT). Advocating self-determination under a Portuguese flag while holding open the door to gradual independence, UDT envisioned ongoing Portuguese developmental assistance for at least another 15 years and drew its support from the network of Timorese chieftains appointed by the colonial administrators. But relying on a colonial infrastructure soon set to vanish, this party from the start was established on a fragile foundation.³

The second party, the Timorese Democratic Popular Association (*Associação Popular Democratica Timorense*, or Apodeti), espoused integration with Indonesia. The leadership of Apodeti was heavily represented by the landed Osorio Soares family, who had a history of ties to Indonesia. One of the Soares siblings, a sergeant in the colonial army, had had an affair with a member of the Indonesian consulate in Dili and was reverse-exiled to Lisbon for the indiscretion. Another of the siblings, Jose, was fired from a colonial administrative job for his pro-Indonesia sympathies; he would later become Apodeti's founder and secretary general.

The third party, the Timorese Social Democratic Association (*Associação Social-Democrata Timorense*, or ASDT), demanded immediate independence. It was led by a pair of Timorese who passed for intellectuals, though both had only modest formal educations. The first was 28-year old Nicolau dos Reis

---

2 As of 1975, there was only one secondary school and less than ten university graduates. "Report by the Secretary-General in Pursuance of Security Council Resolution 384," 12 March 1976, p. 2.
3 UDT founder F.X. Lopes da Cruz advocated Portuguese developmental assistance for another 15-25 years. Interview with F.X. Lopes da Cruz, 29 June 2017.

Lobato, the son of a school teacher and himself a civil servant. The second was Francisco Xavier do Amaral, 37, a Jesuit seminarian who was never ordained and instead went to work at the Dili customs office.

As might be expected given the backgrounds of Lobato and Amaral, the ASDT drew its initial backing from the Timorese civil service. Over the course of a year, however, the party came to be influenced by a handful of radical Timorese students in Lisbon, who in turn stressed the need to court grassroots support. By September 1974, the latter's leftist sway was evident when the ASDT renamed itself as the Revolutionary Front of Independent East Timor (*Frente Revolucionária de Timor-Leste Independente*, or Fretilin).

*

Up until the time these three Timorese parties took shape, Indonesia had only paid scant attention to Portuguese Timor. Sure, the Indonesian intelligence service had occasionally meddled during President Sukarno's administration prior to 1965, but these had been clumsy, half-hearted attempts that were orders of magnitude smaller than Indonesia's interventions in places like Papua and Kalimantan. Portugal would have been forgiven for not over-reacting to these minor provocations, though beginning in 1961 the colonial administrators did see reason to raise a militia (known as *Sekunda Lina*, Portuguese for "Second Line") to augment its frontier defenses with Indonesia's West Timor.[4]

When Suharto took power in 1965, Indonesia arguably paid even less attention to Portugal's colonial outcrop on its periphery. Preoccupied with resuscitating the nation's moribund economy, Suharto seemed to have no interest in the adventurism that characterized his predecessor's government. In fact, the military campaign that dominated the early Suharto years involved cleaning up the paramilitary mess left inside Indonesia's borders on the island of Kalimantan.

But after the Carnation Revolution, Jakarta had little choice but to take heed of developments in the eastern half of Timor. In this case, Indonesia's intelligence service—known as the State Intelligence Coordination Agency (*Badan Koordinasi Intelijen Negara*, or Bakin)—was mandated with leading the response. In the third quarter of 1974, Bakin initiated a multi-pronged operation—codenamed Komodo—intended to woo the emergent crop

---

4   An account of Indonesia's occasional attempts to foster discord in Portuguese Timor can be found in Ernest Chamberlain, *Faltering Steps: Independence Movements in East Timor* in the 1950s and 1960s (Point Lonsdale, Australia, 2005).

of native Timorese politicians from all three parties. This included the disbursement of funds, subsidized soirees in Jakarta, and gray radio broadcasts beamed from West Timor.[5]

As Bakin pushed this soft-sell approach through the beginning of 1975, the political atmosphere in Dili could not have been more cordial. This should have come as little surprise, as the limited vocational and educational opportunities in Timor had led to some fairly incestuous ties between the upper echelons of the three parties. Fretilin's Lobato, for example, was childhood schoolmates with two of the Osorio Soares brothers from Apodeti. Too, Fretilin's Amaral had attended a Macau seminary alongside the head of UDT and yet another of the Osorio Soares brothers; he then married one of the Osorio Soares sisters.

Unfortunately for the Timorese, international events were to conspire against them. On mainland Southeast Asia, communist forces by the second quarter of 1975 had overthrown Western-backed regimes in Cambodia, Laos, and South Vietnam. The Domino Theory was still in currency, with many observers predicting leftist insurgents would steamroll Thailand and possibly more. In Africa, meantime, communist insurgents were on the cusp of seizing power in the former Portuguese territories.

All of this put Suharto and his generals on edge, especially since anti-communism was the mantra of the Jakarta regime. Their concerns were especially focused against Fretilin, which despite its protestations that it was nationalist in outlook and advocated social democracy in the West European sense, was hardly helping its cause by opting to use 'revolutionary' in its name.[6] In response, Bakin's Komodo operation increasingly focused on sowing discord between the Timorese parties, in particular to sour UDT toward any alliance with Fretilin.

At the same time, Portugal's attitude during this period was not especially helpful. Propping up what was effectively a lame-duck colonial administration in Dili, Lisbon had reduced the number of European troops in Timor from 3,000 in 1974 to just over 100 in the summer of 1975. Worse, a pair of leftist MFA majors—Costa Jonatas and Francisco Mota—had arrived in Dili, whereupon they made no secret of their sympathies toward Fretilin; both began helping the pro-independence party spread its grassroots message across the countryside

---

5   The Komodo efforts are detailed in Ken Conboy, *Intel: Inside Indonesia's Intelligence Service* (Jakarta: Equinox Publishing, 2004), pp. 88-90.
6   Fretilin leaders repeatedly tried to play down their leftist slant, and instead highlight their nationalist agenda, in media interviews through 1975. See *Foreign Broadcast Information Service* [hereafter FBIS], Asia and Pacific edition, 3 March 1975, p. Q3.

and especially to Timorese conscripts serving in the colonial military.[7]

Some background on Timor's colonial military is in order. Because the Timorese in the main had been exceedingly loyal and subservient to Portugal, the number of European troops stationed in Timor was always very limited. Indeed, aside from a few technical troops and senior officers, the only purely European units were two artillery companies and a military police company that served two-year tours in Timor. All three of these companies returned permanently to Portugal in the first quarter of 1975, offset somewhat by the arrival of a 60-man paratroop detachment in early April.[8]

Rather than Europeans, the defense forces in Timor were overwhelmingly comprised of native Timorese, with mandatory conscription enforced for most able-bodied males. As of mid-1975, these almost wholly Timorese forces consisted of four 120-man hunter companies, one cavalry group in the border town of Bobonaro numbering 250 men and horses, and a training center at Aileu.[9] There were also some fifty-two companies of *Secunda Lina* militia, which though poorly equipped had the effect of making the countryside awash with firearms.

It was with these forces in place that events spiraled out of control on 11 August 1975. Fearing a Fretilin coup d'état was imminent, armed UDT loyalists during the pre-dawn hours seized the initiative and wrested control of key towns. While UDT was disciplined in Dili, and generally did not mistreat Fretilin supporters, it was a different story in the countryside. Condensed into such a small land mass, family-based vendettas and inter-district rivalries had been festering for generations. When UDT made their power-grab, these personal feuds led to a scattering of bloody reprisals aimed at Fretilin.

Within a week, however, the tables turned. Although UDT was supported by about half the Timorese sergeants in the defense forces, a much larger number of enlisted troops had been drawn to Fretilin's populist themes. Striking back against UDT during a month-long civil war, Fretilin emerged victorious. They also emerged vindictive, unleashing a far wider wave of killings and detentions against both UDT and Apodeti cadre.

By mid-September 1975, the remnants of UDT and Apodeti were

---

7   Jonatas and Mota were ostensibly 'special advisors' to the colonial government, but spent their time taking measures to strengthen Fretilin. Correspondence with Portuguese military historian Luis A.M. Grao, 19 October 1995.

8   Grao correspondence. Australian diplomatic cables at the time incorrectly put the number of Portuguese paratroopers at 400. Wendy Way (ed.), *Australia and the Indonesian Incorporation of Portuguese Timor, 1974-1976* (Melbourne: Melbourne University Press, 2000), pp. 331-333.

9   The four hunter companies, which were akin to light infantry units, were stationed at Maubisse, the Oecusse enclave, Baucau, and Los Palos.

limping toward the Indonesian border. For Apodeti, this was a natural move to seek succor from their benefactors; for UDT, Indonesia now offered the only viable sanctuary. In Dili and much of the countryside, Fretilin was left free to consolidate its hold.

For its part, the Portuguese colonial authorities, effectively abandoned by Lisbon, on 26 August loaded aboard ships in Dili and moved 25 kilometers to nearby *Ilha de Ataúro*—"Island of Goats"—to watch the mayhem from afar.[10] Those making the shift were a paltry few: the military governor, his staff of seven, three military doctors, twenty-six navy men, an air force pilot, and the paratroop detachment.[11] Another 1,000 European refugees—mostly Portuguese—boarded chartered vessels for a boatlift to Darwin. Meanwhile, over 50 Portuguese soldiers were stranded in the interior and were soon taken captive by either UDT or Fretilin.[12]

Before leaving, the Portuguese had done almost nothing to prevent their substantial armories from being looted, with most weapons falling into Fretilin hands. One exception: the paratroopers took the firing pins out of their personal rifles and threw them into the sea to prevent them from being appropriated by the warring parties.[13]

As might be expected, these events had worked Jakarta into a frenzy. Seeing ghosts, in mid-August the Indonesian media printed claims of clandestine Chinese arms shipments to Timor and "Vietnamese terrorists" arriving to help. Other Indonesian media accounts hinted at secret Australian

---

10 On 16 August, Portuguese Major Antonio Joao Soares, an emissary from the Portuguese president, transited Jakarta in an attempt to reach Dili to negotiate with the warring factions. Indonesian intelligence officers surreptitiously gained access to his briefcase during a Bali layover on 17 August, revealing documents from Lisbon that ordered the Portuguese colonial authorities to abandon Dili and retreat to nearby Atauro. Conboy, pp. 91-92. Soares was further delayed by the Indonesian officers, then had his Indonesia visa revoked on 19 August before he could reach Timor. Furious, he returned to Portugal without completing his mission. Way, p. 324.

11 The two left-leaning majors, Jonata and Mota, had already fled to Australia by plane on 17 August. Grao correspondence.

12 Twenty-eight Portuguese soldiers held by Fretilin were soon released and sent to Darwin. Two other Portuguese soldiers who pledged loyalty to the UDT were later captured by Fretilin and executed. Twenty-three more Portuguese soldiers were captured by UDT at Batugede and the Oecussi enclave. On 28 August, a section of Portuguese paratroopers from Atauro boarded a vessel and attempted to release their comrades at Oecussi, but were rebuffed by UDT combatants. These twenty-three soldiers, along with forty-eight Portuguese refugees, were marched across the border to a detention camp inside West Timor during the last quarter of 1975. After prolonged negotiations with Lisbon—and a promise by Portugal to recognize Timor's integration with Indonesia—all were released on 27 July 1976 and flown back to Lisbon. *História Sucinta do Destacamento de Paraquedistas de Timor* (undated), p. 11.

13 *História Sucinta do Destacamento de Paraquedistas de Timor*, p. 8.

arms shipments to Timor and even Australian volunteers fighting alongside Fretilin.[14] By the opening of November, an Indonesian paper alleged that a foreign submarine—nationality unspecified—was spotted off the coast of the Timorese town of Baucau.[15]

That none of these charges were true hardly mattered.[16] Komodo's attempt at social engineering in Portuguese Timor had clearly failed. Worse, by the second week of November Cuba had started openly sending hundreds of troops to Angola to assist communist insurgents vying for control over that former Portuguese colony. Though it was a stretch to draw direct parallels to Timor, the comparison was being made. For Suharto and his top brass, more forceful measures were in order.

---

14 Way, p. 551.
15 Matthew Jardine, *East Timor: Genocide in Paradise* (Tucson: Odonian Press, 1995), p. 29; FBIS, Asia and Pacific edition, 3 November 1975, p. Q1.
16 Though the charges of foreign military assistance appear to be hollow, this was not for want of trying on Fretilin's part. Back in September 1974, a top Fretilin member had secretly written to the Chinese ambassador in Canberra asking for military support and comparing their struggle to North Vietnam and Cambodia. There is no evidence the Chinese responded. Then on 3 December 1975, Fretilin's Amaral wrote to Hanoi asking for help. Again, there is no evidence that Vietnam obliged. Awet Twelde Weldemichael, *Third World Colonialism and Strategies of Liberation: Eritrea and East Timor* (New York: Cambridge University Press, 2013), p. 74.

CHAPTER TWO
SEROJA

Though disappointed with Komodo's inability to shape Portuguese Timor to its will, Jakarta had not exactly been caught flat-footed. At almost the same time that Komodo started, in fact, the Indonesian military began the groundwork for far more aggressive operations inside the Portuguese half of Timor.

Tapped to spearhead that effort was the Indonesian Army's elite Special Warfare Force Command (*Komando Pasukan Sandi Yudha*, or Kopassandha). By way of background, Kopassandha traced its lineage back to 1952 when a small cadre of commandos was raised in West Java province. By the end of the 1950s, it had expanded into an Army Para-Commando Regiment (*Regimen Para-Komando Angkatan Darat*, or RPKAD) with a headquarters at Cijantung hamlet on the southern outskirts of Jakarta.

As its name implicitly stated, the RPKAD was a fast-response airborne commando force that could be quickly dispatched to quell the uprisings that occasionally flared across the Indonesian archipelago. To boost mobility, its members were trained to improvise and subside on a fraction of the logistics required of more lumbering conventional units.

Over the course of the next decade, the RPKAD continued to evolve. The bulk of its members remained focused on the para-commando mission. But a smaller sub-set received additional training based on U.S. Army Special Forces (USSF) doctrine. This doctrine, conjured during the height of the Cold War, stressed a more nuanced unconventional approach in which the Special Forces would act as force-multipliers by raising and advising indigenous guerrillas in the event of being overrun by the Communist Bloc. For this select RPKAD sub-set, their unconventional orientation became known as *sandi yudha*, or 'special warfare.'

As a result of this divided mission, the RPKAD developed two strains of elite solider under its roof. On the one hand, the para-commandos, which stressed physical conditioning and fast assault tactics, were gathered into three brigade-sized groups: Group 1 co-located with the headquarters at Cijantung, Group 2 at the Cental Java city of Magelang, and Group 3 split between the Central Java cities of Solo and Semarang. These groups each consisted of three combat detachments, with a detachment equivalent on paper to a light battalion. Detachments were further sub-divided into companies, platoons, and squads.

On the other hand, the *sandi yudha* members, who tended to be more seasoned and with greater aptitude than their para-commando peers, were gathered under Group 4 at Cijantung. Significantly, Group 4 copied the USSF's structure down to the lowest level. According to the U.S. model, the primarily building block for unconventional warfare operations was the Operational Detachment-A, nicknamed the A-Team. Led by a captain, the A-Team consisted of eleven other members: a deputy commander, an operations sergeant, an assistant operations and intelligence sergeant, two weapons sergeants, two engineering sergeants, two medical sergeants, and two communications sergeants. This structure provided redundancy and facilitated dividing them into two six-man teams while in the field, thus doubling their unconventional warfare coverage if necessary.

Above the A-Teams was the Operational Detachment-B, more commonly known as the B-Team. Consisting of a small headquarters element led by a major, the B-Team controlled half a dozen A-Teams.

Tweaking this formula slightly for the Indonesian context, the basic building block of Group 4 was a twelve-man *prayudha* (from the Sanskrit term meaning 'pre-war'). A close copy of the A-Team, each *prayudha* consisted of a first lieutenant as commander, a deputy commander, an operations sergeant, two intelligence/territorial warfare sergeants, an engineering sergeant, two weapons sergeants, two communications sergeants, and two medics.[1] Like their U.S. counterparts, in theory a *prayudha* could be divided down the middle and sent to different operational areas, doubling their coverage.

Above the *prayudha* in the Group 4 organizational structure was the *karsa yudha*. In Sanskrit, *karsa* means desire or willingness; thus, the *karsa*

---

[1] For the first year, the Group 4 *prayudha* included a logistics sergeant as a thirteenth member. This thirteenth position was soon found to be unnecessary and eliminated.

yudha targeted the enemy's desire to perpetrate a war. A scaled-down version of a USSF B-Team, the *karsa yudha*, led by a captain, consisted of a 24-man headquarters in control of four *prayudha*. As of early 1969, Group 4 had enough men to field three *karsa yudha*.

Almost from the start, Group 4 moved away from the USSF's original raison d'être of raising behind-the-lines guerrillas in the Cold War context. Instead, during initial deployments in places like Papua and Kalimantan, *sandi yudha* teams were tasked with more immediate concerns like counter-insurgency sweeps and gathering combat intelligence. Perhaps sensing that these kinds of duties would be in greater demand in the future, in 1970 it was decided to upgrade Group 3 from para-commandos to a *sandi yudha* group. To reflect this shift toward more unconventional assets, in 1971 the RPKAD was renamed Kopassandha.

It was under this new name that Kopassandha was assigned an initial mission in Portuguese Timor. This began in February 1975, when it was becoming increasingly apparent that Operation Komodo was not having its desire effect. Major General Leonardus Benjamin "Benny" Moerdani, who had emerged as the military's influential intelligence czar, grew impatient and launched a combat intelligence operation codenamed Flamboyan (Indonesian for "Royal Poinciana"). Drawing on Group 4, an augmented *karsa yudha* was deployed to the West Timor border town of Atambua, where it began giving basic paramilitary instruction to Apodeti volunteers that supported integration. Members of this same *karsa yudha* also began making shallow intelligence-gathering forays along the 200-kilometer border into the Portuguese side of the island.

In August 1975, when the UDT putsch sparked a civil war, a wave of UDT and Apodeti partisans soon fled toward the West Timor border and swelled the ranks of the pro-integration Timorese being trained by the Kopassandha *karsa yudha*. By that time, Kopassandha had started giving the callsign '*nanggala*' (after a legendary Hindu spear with multiple points) to all its combat deployments. Given the spreading turmoil in Timor, the *karsa yudha* in Atambua, now codenamed Nanggala 2, was not only busy training guerrillas, but also began clashing with armed Fretilin patrols when it crossed the border during its covert intelligence forays.[2]

By October, with Fretilin seemingly going from strength to strength, General Moerdani quietly approved plans for Flamboyan units to begin a new phase of hit-and-run strikes. Arriving to participate were two more

---

2   A mid-1975 deployment of a *karsa yudha* to Papua was callsigned Nanggala 1.

Kopassandha detachments—dubbed Nanggala 3 and 4—each consisting of two *prayudha* and two para-commando platoons.

The purpose of this new phase of raids was as a prelude to something far bigger. Back on 31 August, in fact, before the dust in the Timorese civil war had even settled, the commander of the Indonesian Armed Forces had created a Combined Task Force Command (*Komando Tugas Gabungan*, or Kogasgab) that would secretly plan, organize and, more than likely, execute a massive combined arms invasion to seize control of Portuguese Timor.

The top Kogasgab leadership was packed with officers from elite units. The commander, Brigadier General Chamid Soeweno, was head of the Kopassandha training center. His intelligence assistant, Colonel Dading Kalbuadi, was another Kopassandha officer concurrently in charge of the Flamboyan operation. The head of ground operations was a long-time airborne officer, Colonel Muhammad Sanif, while the head of airborne operations, Colonel Rudini, was previously in charge of an airborne infantry brigade.

In mid-October, Soeweno began issuing orders to the small but growing number of military assets being shifted to Kogasgab control in West Timor. Though this was dubbed a defensive phase of operations, it was anything but. On 15 October, for example, a battalion from Infantry Brigade 2 from East Java was ordered to edge into Portuguese Timor and occupy the border towns of Maliana, Bobonaro, and Lebos. The following morning, the infantrymen easily overran Maliana—but were firmly rebuffed at Lebos. The day after that, they started moving on Bobonaro, but again were kept at bay by tenacious Fretilin defenders.[3]

The glacial gains registered by Infantry Brigade 2 were the rule rather than the exception during Kogasgab's early efforts. Unfazed, Soeweno's staff forged ahead with ambitious plans for a blitz near year's end. Planning for this, in fact, predated the establishment of Kogasgab by six months, when a small Kopassandha team was tasked by General Moerdani to pen a theoretical ground offensive that would steamroll from the West Timor border all the way to the eastern tip of the island.

Very quickly, the planners discounted the idea of a plodding ground operation and instead focused on an airborne assault. By April 1975, they had gone as far as creating a crude diorama of Dili in the Cijantung mess so that the para-commandos could familiarize themselves with the city's layout.[4]

---

3   *Laporan Operasi Seroja*, Komando Daerah Militer VIII Brawijaya, Brigade Infanteri 2 KTD-AD, p. 2.
4   Interview with Theo Syafei, one of the Kopassandha planners, 9 July 2005.

Planning was put on hold that same month—because President Suharto did not want to spark controversy during an official visit to Australia—but resumed with a vengeance after the Timorese civil war broke out in August. By then, the Kopassandha planners, now merged under Kogasgab, were continuously fine-tuning their anticipated airborne assault. Kogasgab was initially assigned 500 para-commandos divided into two combat detachments—one each from Group 1 and 2—for what was being dubbed Operation Seroja (Indonesian for "Lotus"). Codenamed Nanggala 5, the two combat detachments would be led by the Group 1 commander, Lieutenant Colonel Soegito.[5]

Very quickly, Seroja was hit by changes. With Kogasgab assets meeting heavier-than-anticipated Fretilin resistance along the border, half of Nanggala 5 was stripped away and sent as reinforcements on the West Timor frontier. With Nanggala 5 reduced by fifty percent, the Seroja planners augmented the envisioned Dili assault force with two airborne infantry battalions.

With the additional of the airborne battalions, Seroja looked impressive on paper. Its opening maneuver was to be massive parachute jump, one of the largest single-day drops attempted since World War Two.[6] By a wide margin, it was also the largest combat jump ever contemplated by the Indonesian Armed Forces.[7] But this plan was less than ideal because tactical command and control was now spread between two parent organizations—Kopassandha and the airborne infantry—neither of which was given jurisdiction over the other. Too, operational secrecy prevented any dress rehearsals among them.

There was another key variable outside the military's control. Ever since consolidating control in Dili in September 1975, Fretilin had been moving to form a rudimentary government in all but name. Plans were afoot to officially declare independence in early December; however, after Indonesia telegraphed its intent with a steady increase in border incursions, the Fretilin leadership moved forward its timetable and on 28 November announced the establishment

---

5   In keeping with the floral theme after Flamboyan and Seroja, Bakin penned plans for a program called *Melati* (Indonesian for "Jasmine") that involved social engineering in the fields of education and economics to be conducted in the years immediately after an Indonesian occupation of Timor. But after Bakin came to be over-shadowed by the military in Timor, Melati never got past the planning stage.

6   The largest one-day drop in history was during World War Two, when more than 16,000 U.S. and British paratroopers jumped into Germany during Operation Varsity in March 1945. The largest post-War jump involved 3,437 U.S. paratroopers and a 12-man Indian medical team that jumped during the Korean War in March 1951. The next largest one-day post-War jump involved 1,188 British and French paratroopers during the 1956 Suez crisis.

7   The largest single-day drop by Indonesia to that time had been during Operation Naga in West New Guinea during 1962. This involved 56 RPKAD members and a 160-man airborne infantry company.

of the Democratic Republic of East Timor. The two Fretilin founders, Lobato and Amaral, were named prime minister and president, respectively. The first article of their independence declaration made clear their anti-colonialist, anti-neocolonialist, and anti-imperialist outlook; such revolutionary wording, naturally, only served to harden the resolve of Indonesia's generals.[8]

By that late hour, Fretilin no doubt figured an Indonesian invasion was inevitable and they had nothing to lose by declaring independence. And they would have been right. Kogasgab had already quietly issued an operational order which set D-Day for 7 December, with Dili being the first and most important target, Baucau (with the longest runway in Portuguese Timor) the next, and Aileu (which hosted the colonial military training center) the third. Seven more towns fleshed out the target list, though these were to be tackled at unspecified later dates.[9]

Back at Cijantung, Nanggala 5 assembled on 5 December for their final Seroja briefing. What they heard reeked of optimism: their mission would be finished within three days, and they would be back in Jakarta no later than February. So confident was the chain-smoking Soegito that he would later give prominent place in his rucksack to cartons of cigarettes instead of extra ammunition.

The following night, General Maraden Panggabean, who wore the twin hats of Armed Forces Commander and Minister of Defense and Security, was at the forward Kogasgab command post at Penfui airbase near Kupang. Perhaps sensing that confidence was unrealistically high, he hedged somewhat. "He told us to expect 35 percent casualties during the Dili operation," remembered one Kogasgab staff member who was present. Panggabean also repeated the bromide that Indonesia would never allow a Cuba on its border.[10]

When the jump did take place the following dawn, it resulted in the largest number of fatalities the Indonesian military ever suffered during a single day of combat since independence. Among the Nanggala 5 members, fourteen were killed by Fretilin gunfire, three more landed in the water off Dili and drowned, and two others were missing (their bodies were found months

---

8 To offset Fretilin's independence declaration, the Indonesian government two days later hurriedly arranged for pro-integration Timorese parties to sign a document deriding the Fretilin declaration and providing a legal fig leaf for the Seroja invasion. Besides signatories from Apodeti and UDT, two other exceedingly small Timorese parties that barely rated as a footnote—KOTA, which purported to represent traditional tribal royalty, and Trabalhista, which claimed to advocate for Timorese laborers—also signed the document.

9 *Laporan Pelaksanaan Tugas Operasi Kogasgab* "S," Departemen Pertahanan dan Keamanan, 8 February 1976, p. 10.

10 Syafei interview.

later). Among the airborne infantry, some thirty-six paratroopers were killed in combat. So intense was the gunfire by Fretilin defenders that a third and final airborne sortie was cancelled.[11]

Three days later, a joint force of Kopassandha (totaling sixty-five Nanggala 5 commandos who had been on the aborted third sortie at Dili) and elements of an airborne infantry brigade jumped to seize Baucau. Unlike the Dili airborne assault, Fretilin had already abandoned Baucau and pragmatically melted into the jungle to fight another day. The paratroopers, as a result, did not face a human enemy; dozens, however, were severely injured from sharp boulders that peppered the drop-zone.

Shortly thereafter, the commandos from Baucau were sent to reunite with the bulk of Nanggala 5 still in Dili. At full strength, Nanggala 5 was then used to spearhead the government's push southwest toward their third target, Aileu.

What came next was a rude foreshadowing of things to come. For the entire twenty-four kilometers, largely unseen Timorese combatants picked away at the Indonesian column and slowed them to a crawl.

That the Timorese were showing this level of tenacity should not have been a surprise. Indeed, the armed wing of Fretilin, going by the name Armed Forces for the National Liberation of East Timor (*Forças Armadas da Libertação Nacional de Timor-Leste*, or Falintil), had for the past several months repeatedly proven their mettle. Created back in August 1975 during the counter-coup against UDT, the backbone of the 30,000-man Falintil were the former Timorese members of the colonial defense force (known in Portuguese as *Tropas*, or 'Troops'). The *Tropas* were hardly novices to warfare: the Portuguese had enforced three months of military training for most Timorese males, after which they were obliged to enlist in *Tropas* for three years. Over the year since the Carnation Revolution, they had even started recruiting from high school and allowing more Timorese to become non-commissioned officers. Those completing their three years of compulsory service were given the option of transferring from *Tropas* to the *Sekunda Lina* militia.[12]

The result was that most Timorese males had at least a modicum of

---

11   Had the third sortie gone as planned, the Seroja jump at Dili would have totaled around 1,200 men and ranked as the second largest single-day airborne assault since World War Two. With the cancellation of the third sortie, however, just over 900 men participated and the operation ranked as the third largest post-War jump. Hendro Subroto, *Operasi Udara di Timor Timur* (Jakarta: Pustaka Sinar Harapan, 2005), p. 156.

12   Prior to 1974 only a handful of Timorese had become non-commissioned officers or lieutenants. Five (including two ethnic Chinese and one ethnic Arab) had experience in Africa, while another three were trained in Portugal. Lopes da Cruz interview; interview with Vidal Sarmento, 21 June 2016.

military discipline and skills. Moreover, the bulk of *Tropas* had pledged loyalty to Falintil, as had an overwhelming 90 percent of *Sekunda Lina* militiamen. In addition, Falintil had given a week's worth of paramilitary training to 1,000 junior high and high school students in Dili just prior to the Seroja invasion.[13]

For Falintil, too, firearms and ammunition were plentiful. Former *Tropas* combatants were equipped with the NATO-standard G-3 assault rifle, which the Indonesians nicknamed the 'Getme.' Based on a German design and produced by Portugal during the 1950s in collaboration with Spain, the Getme used a 20-round clip and had an effective range of 500 meters.[14] There were an estimated 15,000 Getme rifles in Timor as of the August breakdown in law and order, the vast majority falling into Falintil hands.[15]

The former *Sekunda Lina*, meantime, were equipped with thousands of Mauser bolt-action rifles. An antiquated design that had been the German service rifle in the 1930s, it nevertheless packed a strong punch out to 500 meters.

For heavier weapons, Falintil had taken possession of forty 60mm mortars, twenty 81mm mortars, twenty 3.5-inch rocket launchers, a sizable number of FBP 9 submachine guns, as well as the the MG 34 German machine gun.[16] They also took control of six 75mm howitzers and dozens of jeeps and Unimog utility vehicles, some of which were used as mobile mortar platforms.

With these numbers, training, and weaponry, Falintil made the Indonesians pay dearly during the slog toward Aileu. Averaging four kilometers a day for six days, Nanggala 5 finally pushed its way into the former *Tropas* training center on 29 December. Again, Failintil had already pragmatically melted away to fight another day. "No civilians were present," recalled one

---

13 Interview with Sera Malik, 29 June 2005. Australian diplomatic cables estimated Falintil had about 30,000 members as of early December 1975. Of these, 3,000 were the *Tropas* core, while the remainder were poorly-trained militia. Way, p. 499.
14 The nickname 'Getme' was based on a misunderstanding compounded by a mispronunciation. The Portuguese G-3 was originally developed in collaboration with the Spanish state-owned *Centro da Estudios Técnicos de Materiales Especiales* (CETME). Although the Portuguese-made version was distinct from that produced in Spain, the Indonesians fixated on the CETME connection. Mispronouncing this as 'Getme,' this incorrect nickname entered the Indonesian military's vernacular. Correspondence with Antonio E.S. Carmo, 16 February 2002.
15 Way, op. cit., p. 384. A far higher estimate of 29,000 G-3s is given by Francisco Osorio Soares, who served in the administrative section of *Tropas* through 1975 and helped calculate weapon inventories. Interview with Francisco Osorio Soares, 9 August 2016.
16 *Laporan Singkat*, Timor-Leste Armed Violence Assessment, No. 1, October 2008, p. 4. Given the prior close relationship between Germany and the fascist regime in Lisbon, many of these weapons were either purchased decades earlier from Germany—like the Mauser and MG 34—or based on German designs, like the Getme and FBP 9.

Kopassandha officer. "Except the Chinese shopkeepers: they always stayed."[17]

*

Although Kogasgab had consolidated control over its top three targets two days before year's end, there was hardly reason for cheer. After all not only was Falintil proving to be far more determined than anticipated, but Seroja had not happened in a vacuum. While the Indonesian authorities were doing their best to control media coverage, or lack thereof, information about the invasion was leaking out. The international community had taken notice, and their scrutiny was putting Jakarta in a bad light.

Stoking this critical reaction was Indonesia's bête noire, a pugnacious Timorese named Jose Ramos-Horta. Born in mountainous Laklubar sub-district of Mestizo ancestry, Ramos-Horta had rebellion in his blood. His grandfather was an anarchist bomb thrower in Portugal, resulting in his exile to Timor in 1927. His father was also a deportado, expelled from Portugal in the late 1930s after he tried to fight fascists in the Spanish Civil War. Continuing the family tradition in reverse, Ramos-Horta as a teen was exiled from Timor to Mozambique in 1970 after making subversive anti-colonial statements.

Back in Portuguese Timor during the Carnation Revolution, Ramos-Horta quickly gravitated toward Fretilin's pro-independence platform. Showing aptitude and intensity—and a propensity for channeling Che Guevarra as he flitted about Dili in army fatigues, bloused boots, and an untidy beard—he rose to the top of the youthful Fretilin leadership. When the Democratic Republic of East Timor was founded in late November 1975, he was named Minister for Foreign Relations and Information.

By that late hour, an Indonesian invasion looked imminent. Realizing he could make a bigger impact on the international circuit, on 4 December Ramos-Horta boarded one of the last planes out of Timor and flew to Darwin to meet with a small but vibrant community of Fretilin sympathizers. He was still there when Seroja launched on 7 December.

As Fretilin's senior foreign envoy at the tender age of twenty-five, Ramos-Horta soon was winging his way to Lisbon, then the United Nations headquarters in New York. On 12 December, the day after he arrived in Manhattan, the UN General Assembly began consideration on the Timor issue. With help from countries like China, Tanzania, and Guyana, Ramos-Horta, trading in khaki fatigues for a jacket and tie, tirelessly worked the diplomatic

---

17 Syafei interview.

scene to engender sympathy for the Timorese. The result of his efforts during a subsequent General Assembly vote was mixed: 59 nations deplored Indonesia's military intervention, 11 countries did not, and 55 countries—primarily from the West—chose to abstain.

From the General Assembly, the Timor issue on 15 December shifted to the UN Security Council. One week later, this select 15-member group unanimously called on the immediate withdrawal of the Indonesian invasion force and respect for Timorese self-determination. According to the UN Charter, all member states—which included Indonesia and Portugal—were obliged to comply with such Security Council resolutions.

Significantly, the Security Council also called on the UN Secretary-General to urgently send a special envoy to "make an on-the-spot assessment and establish contact with all parties in the Territory and all the States concerned in order to ensure the full implementation of the resolution."[18]

Austria's Kurt Waldheim, who had taken over as the UN's fourth Secretary-General in 1972, was immediately informed of this directive. Fortunately for Waldheim, he did not have to ponder long over his choice of a proven troubleshooter who could handle a sensitive fact-finding mission in Timor. Waiting until after Christmas and the long holiday weekend, on 29 December he placed a call to Vittorio Winspeare in Geneva.

---

18   "Report by the Secretary-General in Pursuance of Security Resolution 384," p. 1.

CHAPTER THREE
PITBULL IN PINSTRIPES

To see Vittorio Winspeare walking the grounds of the UN office in Geneva, one might sense a hint of nobility about the tall, bespectacled diplomat. And one would be right. His family traced back a recusant Catholic family of English origin who, rebuffing pressure to join the Church of England, moved in the Eighteenth Century to the Kingdom of Naples in the southern part of the Italian peninsula.

In Naples, the Winspeares married into the local aristocracy and thrived. Over the course of a century, successive generations produced noted judges, a mayor of Naples, and several generals that served under various flags. With their noble status, too, came land; the family quickly amassed a staggering catalog of properties around Naples, including the Sixteenth Century Acquaviva d'Atri palace.

By the time Baron Vittorio Winspeare was born in Sicily in 1912, his birthright all but guaranteed a cloistered life of wealth and privilege. But nobody could accuse this Winspeare of taking it easy. First getting an undergraduate education in economics from prestigious Bocconi University, he then earned a law degree from the University of Turin. After that he became the first in his family to join Italy's Foreign Office and was dispatched as a junior diplomat to South America.

It was there that the turmoil of World War Two caught up with the young baron. While serving at the Italian embassy in Rio de Janeiro, he was summarily arrested in August 1942 after Brazil belatedly declared war on the Axis powers. Bundled off to a U.S. detainment camp for several months, he was then shipped to Sweden in a trade for Allied prisoners.

By the time Winspeare set foot back in Europe, vast changes had taken place. On a personal level, a decree by Italy's royalty in January 1943 reconfirmed his family's noble status by authorizing the Winspeares to add the Guicciardi surname.[1] But more critically, his homeland was in turmoil with Allied troops landing in Sicily and Nazi divisions propping up Benito Mussolini's fascist dictatorship in Rome. Sensing the tide of battle was turning, the Fascist Grand Council in July sacked Mussolini, allowing General Pietro Badoglio to slip away to the city of Brindisi and in September sign an armistice with the Allies.

With history quickly unfolding, the baron stole a car and wound his way down to Brindisi. Offering his services to the Badoglio government, he spent the remainder of the war on discrete diplomatic assignments around Italy and North Africa.

Remaining with the Foreign Office after World War Two, Winspeare first served in the London embassy through 1949, then the Bonn embassy through 1954. Rising through the ranks, in 1961 he was named ambassador to Ireland.

The Dublin years proved to be the calm before the storm. In 1966, Winspeare was cross-posted to Prague as head of the Italian mission to Czechoslovakia. In January 1968, he was on hand when reformist Alexander Dubcek was elected First Secretary of that country's communist party. Almost immediately, Dubcek began attempts at political liberalization and economic decentralization in what came to be known at the Prague Spring. The Soviets did not take kindly to these reforms and in August mobilized half a million Warsaw Pact troops to invade the country. Winspeare packed up his family and were on the last train out before the Soviet-led military forces occupied Czechoslovakia in a day and brutally crushed the Prague Spring.[2]

His Czech assignment cut short, Winspeare next was seconded by the Italian Foreign Office to serve at the UN. As luck would have it, the plum role of Director General for the UN Office at Geneva had just become vacant. Situated at the picturesque Palace of Nations compound on the shore of Lake Geneva, it was the second largest of the UN's four major worldwide offices. Overseeing some two dozen constituent agencies, Winspeare was named Director General in Geneva as well as the additional title of Under-Secretary-General.[3]

---

[1] The family's royal status was originally decreed in 1808, though the addition of the Guicciardi surname (and the title of counts) did not come until 1943. Correspondence with Baron Antonio Winspeare Guicciardi, 25 October 2016.

[2] *Ibid.*

[3] Winspeare shunned use of his Guicciardi surname while at the UN. "Winspeare liked to be

As it turned out, Winspeare made an early impression on the UN's Secretary-General, the highly regarded Burmese diplomat U Thant. The two forged immediate chemistry, leading U Thant to recommend his Italian colleague for a particularly sensitive assignment. Back in January 1968, the British had announced they would phase out their remaining colonial outcrops from the Middle East by the end of 1971. This directly impacted their protectorate of Bahrain, a small Arab monarchy in the Persian Gulf. While tiny in size, Bahrain occupied a strategic corner in a tense neighborhood; there was obvious concern over how it would be governed in the post-British vacuum.

The stakes, really, could not be overstated. The Cold War was simmering just below boil, and while Washington might otherwise have filled the void, the U.S. was largely consumed by its military engagements in Southeast Asia.

Complicating matters was Iran's claim that Bahrain was historically theirs. As far back as 1928, the Shah of Iran had written to the League of Nations to state that Bahrain, with rare exception, had been part of the Persian Empire for centuries. Since 1957, in fact, Iran had called Bahrain their fourteen province and reserved a seat for them in parliament.

And then there were the Bahrainis themselves. The majority were Shiite Muslims, like Iran. But there was strong anecdotal evidence to suggest local leaders wanted full independence in the wake of Britain's departure.

After some initial attempts to negotiate an outcome fell flat, the British, Iranians, and Bahrainis agreed to UN mediation. The UN was not to hold or supervise an independence referendum; rather, they were being asked to conduct field inquiries to gauge the wishes of the Bahraini people. In March 1970, U Thanh announced he was dispatching Winspeare as his personal envoy to handle the delicate task.

Over the following month the Under-Secretary-General met with a cross section of Bahraini society, from royalty to street vendors. By all accounts, he tackled his mission with an unbiased hand. When he turned over his findings to the UN Security Council on 30 April, Winspeare was unflinching in his conclusion: the overwhelming majority of residents wished to be fully independent.

Sufficiently persuaded by the report, the Security Council endorsed it in less than two weeks. Convinced, too, was Iran, which dropped its claim to Bahrain two days later. The Bahrainis would go on to get their independence

---

known as such," recalled one of his closest assistants, Erik Jensen. "When we travelled on mission he always asked that I convey to those we met that he preferred to be addressed as Mister Winspeare (without the Guicciardi)." Correspondence with Erik Jensen, 14 January 2017.

in a year.

His first major UN assignment an unqualified success, Winspeare returned to Geneva with his reputation burnished. Not surprisingly, U Thant turned to him again the following year to handle another crisis farther east. In South Asia, tension had been building for months. Specifically, there were growing divisions within Pakistani society, exacerbated by the fact that the nation was physically divided on two sides of India. The eastern side—appropriately known as East Pakistan—had grown resentful of having its administration dominated by those hailing from the west. India, more than happy to heap stress on its sworn enemy, had initiated support to an armed separatist proxy within East Pakistan.

Finally, on 3 December 1971 India and Pakistan began a direct military confrontation. The Indians and separatists steamrolled the East Pakistani forces in days and on 16 December established the independent nation of Bangladesh.

Problems were only starting, however. In addition to the ongoing bad blood between India and Pakistan, millions of Bangladeshis were without sufficient food and proper shelter. Facing a humanitarian nightmare, U Thant on 26 December announced he would immediately send Winspeare as his special envoy to seek a solution for the humanitarian problems impacting the subcontinent.

What came next was a case study in shuttle diplomacy. In the first week of January 1972 alone, the Under-Secretary-General visited the capitals of Bangladesh, India, and Pakistan in quick succession. On 13 January, he was again working his way through starving crowds in the Bangladeshi capital, then headed once more to Pakistan. While there were no easy answers to the humanitarian dilemma in Bangladesh—in fact, famine conditions peaked in 1974, killing an estimated 1.5 million—he had once against shown his tact on the international stage.

By the time Winspeare returned to his office in Geneva, he had a new boss in New York. His ally and mentor, U Thant, had retired on the final day of 1971 after completing two terms. In as the new Secretary-General was Kurt Waldheim. From the outset, the two shared none of the trust and comradery that Winspeare enjoyed with U Thant; indeed, his ties with Waldheim were strained more often than not. Still, he headed the short list of UN troubleshooters with a proven ability to tackle the most complex diplomatic knots. So when Waldheim needed a hard-nosed envoy for the Timor crisis, it came as no surprise when Winspeare landed the assignment.

Arriving in New York on 5 January 1976, Winspeare reported to Waldheim and immediately got to work assembling his fact-finding delegation. Making the cut as special assistant was Erik Jensen, an Oxford-educated Malaysian national of Danish ancestry who was his *chef de cabinet* in Geneva; the two had previously worked together on the Bahrain and Bangladesh assignments. Chosen as political officer was Gilberto Schlitter-Silva (a Brazilian national whose Portuguese language skills were a strong asset), while Norwegian Harald Smaage was added as administrative assistant.

While in New York, Winspeare also used the time to meet with relevant diplomats. On the same day he arrived, he discussed scheduling and administrative details with the Indonesian ambassador. His initial plan called for a visit to Jakarta, followed by a visit to Timor, then another short follow-up visit to Jakarta.

The next morning, he met with Fretilin envoy Jose Ramos-Horta. The combative Ramos-Horta spoke confidently of Fretilin controlling 80 percent of the Timorese countryside and urged the envoy to venture into the hinterlands to meet with the Fretilin leadership. Amenable to the idea, Winspeare pressed for the name of a Timorese airfield where he could have the tryst. Ramos-Horta, for the moment, had no ready reply.[4]

Later that same afternoon, Winspeare met the Australian ambassador to the UN. The ambassador was in tough spot. Canberra valued its cordial ties with Jakarta. At the same time, there was no denying a strong wave of pro-Fretilin and anti-Indonesia sentiment in Australian society: in early October 1975, students had briefly occupied the bottom floor of the Indonesian embassy during a protest; later that same month the union representing Australian dockworkers had declared a ban on servicing Indonesian vessels. Walking a tightrope, the Australian government had declared its support for the UN's fact-finding mission, but preferred to avoid direct involvement. When Winspeare brought up the possibility of chartering an Australian plane to take him from Indonesia into Timor, Canberra gently suggested he look for other options.

The following evening, the Under-Secretary-General flew to Lisbon. The Portuguese were still trying to claim relevance in the debate, this despite the fact that on 9 December they had loaded their residual presence on Atauro aboard two Portuguese navy corvettes and steamed directly to Darwin. The last military governor, Colonel Mário Lemos Pires, was already back in Lisbon and spoke with the UN envoy, as did the Minister for Foreign Affairs and Minister for External Cooperation. All pledged support with a view toward

---

4   Way, p. 673.

free self-determination in Timor. From Lisbon, Winspeare then returned to Geneva for more talks with Indonesian and Portuguese representatives.

As this was happening, Jakarta was fretting over the impending fact-finding mission. They had already set up a Provisional Government of East Timor (PGET) on 17 December, which in turn made a public appeal for Indonesian military, political and economic assistance. This gave Indonesia what they saw as legal cover for their role in Timor, though they were pushing the weak fiction that only Indonesian 'volunteers' were fighting inside the former Portuguese territory.

To ensure they were ready for Winspeare's delegation, Indonesian Foreign Minister Adam Malik on 8 January made a lightning visit to Dili, Atauro, and Baucau. During the same timeframe, U.S. intelligence intercepted messages that the PGET was being coached by Indonesian officials on replies to likely questions, and that efforts were underway to conceal the presence of Indonesian troops and equipment, as well as to repair damage to Dili. In particular, Indonesian Air Force personnel in Timor were being directed to stay away from Timorese airfields while the envoy was present.[5]

Not until 13 January did the PGET send a formal message to Winspeare in Geneva that they were prepared to receive him. Coincidentally, that same day Winspeare also got a cable from a Fretilin information officer in Australia offering to set up a visit via Australia to Fretilin leaders in the Timorese countryside. As with the Ramos-Horta proposal in New York, it was short on logistical specifics.[6]

Two days later, Winspeare arrived at Jakarta's Halim Perdanakusuma airport. The following morning, he and his team began a delicate dance of courtesy calls to President Suharto and Malik. During the latter, Malik strongly advised them to go on a limited tour of Dili, Atauro, Baucau—all of which Malik had helped prepare the previous week—as well as the Oecussi enclave.[7] The envoy agreed, though he insisted on chartering a Twin Otter aircraft so as not be appear beholden to the Indonesian government for transportation to Timor.[8]

After spending the weekend in Jakarta, Winspeare departed for Penfui airbase near Kupang on 19 January. Making short hops in the Twin Otter the next day, he landed at Oecussi, then Atauro, then Dili near nightfall. The following morning the delegation held an initial round of talks with PGET

---

5 "The Timor Papers," *The National Times* (Australia), 6-12 June 1982, p. 34.
6 "Report by the Secretary-General in Pursuance of Security Council Resolution 384," p. 6.
7 FBIS, Asia and Pacific, 15 January 1976, p. Q1.
8 Way, p. 665.

leaders, after which they took a chopper 64 kilometers east to the coastal town of Manatuto. From there they choppered another 58 kilometers east to Baucau, then were back in Dili by dusk. A second round of talks with PGET officials took place on the morning of 22 January, after which the envoy and his team concluded their tour and took the Twin Otter to Bali for the night.[9]

Winspeare's impressions during his three days in Timor were vivid. In the Oecussi enclave he was shocked by the primitive conditions, noting that there were barely any perceivable changes after 500 years of Portuguese rule. He also came away feeling Ramos-Horta's boast about Fretilin controlling 80 percent of the territory rang hollow: the PGET appeared to have a firm grip over the towns and had elements of a working civil service, while the countryside was largely an area of "non-control" by either side.[10]

It was in Dili that the fact-finding team found the scene bordering on the surreal. Not a single Indonesian solider was in sight, nor was much battle damage evident aside from some bullet pockmarks.[11] PGET officials were occupying the former Portuguese governor's office and were ostensibly in charge; this included self-styled "Governor" Arnaldo dos Reis Araujo, a 63-year old Apodeti leader who had been a Japanese collaborator during World War Two and spent a stint in a Portuguese prison cell. Despite Indonesian coaching, the PGET leaders appeared naive and woefully ignorant about the purpose of the Winspeare delegation. They did, however, make clear their desire to merge with Indonesia, their opposition to any independence referendum, and their unwillingness to host a delegation from the UN's Special Committee on Decolonization because there was "no more colonization problem in East Timor." [12]

---

9   Bakin had been pressing its US counterpart, the Central Intelligence Agency, for insights into Timor and the UN fact-finding team, though very little had been forthcoming. On 21 January, however, while Winspeare was in Timor, the CIA station in Jakarta handed over to Bakin two short reports with biodata on Winspeare and his deputy, Erik Jensen. The first report concluded that Winspeare was "even-handed and objective in his official duties." Bakin case file "Portuguese Timor," Biodata on Vittorio Winspeare and Erik Jensen, 21 January 1976.
10 Way, p. 673. When the delegation went to Atauro, they were greeted by a Timorese wearing a naval uniform—apparently part of Indonesia's attempt to convince Winspeare that the PGET was beginning to handle maritime defense responsibilities.
11 "I can confirm the apparent absence of Indonesian military personnel—at least of uniformed personnel," said the delegation's special assistant, Erik Jensen. "It was indeed surprising in the circumstances, but a rather compact program of meetings precluded much wandering around [Dili], and I do not think Winspeare saw the need to act against security advice." Jensen correspondence.
12 FBIS, Asia and Pacific edition, 23 January 1976, p. Q2.

All the while meetings in Dili were taking place, Indonesia's stage-managing was evident. Crowds of locals obediently materialized outside the governor's office whenever the delegation arrived, most waving Indonesian flags. Several held aloft placards in English stating, 'UN envoy has come too late, East Timor has already merged with Indonesia.' Other banners ominously warned, 'Talk little and go quickly.'[13]

Early on 23 January, Winspeare and his team were back in Jakarta. The special envoy admitted to waiting reporters that it seemed he had arrived late and that East Timor had de facto integrated with Indonesia. He also announced his intent to head back to New York three days hence in order to report his findings to Secretary-General Waldheim.[14]

Hearing of this, Indonesia's military and civilian leadership breathed a sigh of relief. Such sentiment was premature, however. This was because awaiting Winspeare in Jakarta was yet another cable, this from the Secretary-General's office saying the envoy had been invited by Fretilin to fly to the Same airstrip inside Timor and meet with Fretilin members in the towns of Suai, Viqueque, and Com. The invitation (prepared by Ramos-Horta in New York) included the name and phone number of a Fretilin officer in Darwin, Tony Belo, who would allegedly arrange the flight to Same.[15]

This latest proposal closely matched the cable Winspeare received in Geneva on 13 January, only now there were some specifics. Three of the locations—Suai, Same, and Viqueque—ran from west to east along the southern half of the island, while Com was a beach on the northeastern corner of Timor.

Winspeare was now in a quandary. His mandate was to talk to all the involved parties, but he had yet to meet any Fretilin member inside Timor.[16] At the same time, any such attempt to fly into the Timorese hinterland was fraught with danger given the fighting raging across the countryside.

The next night, 24 January, Winspeare called Belo in Darwin. Their conversation served up more questions than answers. There was obviously going to be a transportation problem, as it was far from clear what aircraft and aircrew would take them from Darwin into Timor. There was also a communications problem, as Belo was only getting sporadic radio transmissions, often with dated information, from Fretilin jungle redoubts.

---

13 FBIS, Asia and Pacific edition, 23 January 1976, p. Q1; Way, p. 703.
14 FBIS, Asia and Pacific edition, 23 January 1976, p. Q2; 26 January 1976, p. M1.
15 Way, p. 673.
16 A man claiming to be a Fretilin member had materialized during their visit to Manatuto and professed his support for integration with Indonesia. It was later learned he was a Fretilin defector and certainly did not speak for the party.

Things only grew more complicated the next day. For one thing, Canberra reiterated it would not permit the use of an Australian plane for a mission into the Timorese countryside. For another thing, Australian police and telecommunications officials that morning seized Belo's transmitter because he was operating without a license. In doing so, the main communications channel to the besieged Fretilin leadership inside Timor was lost.[17]

His patience wearing thin, Winspeare elected to remain in Jakarta a few more days in order to allow Fretilin representatives in Darwin more time to sort out logistics. In comments to the media, he revealed that consideration was being given to landing at the Same runway. He also said consideration was being given to using one of the Portuguese corvettes berthed at Darwin to land his team along Timor's southern coast, possibly near the beachside town of Betano.[18]

For the Indonesian government, Winspeare's renewed attempts to arrange transportation into East Timor were cause for tremendous concern. From Winspeare's own public statements, they were well aware he was contemplating a meeting with Fretilin at Same or Betano; through confidential sources, they also knew of the proposed meeting sites at Suai, Viqueque, and Com.[19] Trouble was, Seroja was making slow progress and most of these towns had been deemed lower priorities which had yet to be occupied by the Indonesian military; in fact, Same and Betano had been overlooked on the initial target list.[20]

In order to deny the UN delegation any of these landing sites, the generals went into overdrive. On 24 January, an airborne battalion marched into Viqueque with little opposition. Three days later, an infantry battalion was landed largely unopposed by ship at Betano, then began walking north

---

17 Way, p. 673; FBIS, Asia and Pacific edition, 26 January 1976, p. M1; Timor Information Service, No. 7, 1 February 1976.
18 FBIS, Asia and Pacific edition, 27 January 1976, p. M1; 28 January 1976, p. N2.
19 According to the memoir of one Kopassandha officer involved in Seroja, Indonesian 'intelligence sources' learned in late January that Winspeare intended to go to Suai. It is not difficult to imagine how this information was obtained. For one thing, Winspeare had discussed the various meeting sites during his 24 January telephone call to Belo in Darwin, and Indonesian intelligence agencies were rather well-versed in telephone tap operations. For another thing, Winspeare on the morning of 24 January openly discussed details of the Fretilin proposal with the Australian ambassador to Indonesia; it is possible the ambassador may have subsequently mentioned these details with Indonesian counterparts. Subabyo H.S., *Menyabung Nyawa demi Bangsa dan Negara* (Jakarta: Selaras Bintang Media, 2012) p. 44; Way, p. 673.
20 In Kogasgab's initial list of ten targets, Viqueque was number six, Los Palos (adjacent to Com) was number seven, and Suai was number ten. *Laporan Pelaksanaan Tugas Operasi Kogasgab "S,"* p. 10.

toward Same.[21]

The heightened tempo of Indonesian military operations was not lost on Winspeare. But offsetting these developments, the Portuguese by 29 January appeared increasingly willing to land the UN party from one of their corvettes staging out of Darwin. The Portuguese also appeared amenable to letting Fretilin coordinate with their colleagues inside Timor via the radio on one of their warships in lieu of Tony Belo's seized transmitter. With transportation and communications suddenly looking more feasible, Winspeare hinted at shifting his delegation to Darwin within a few short days.[22]

Not surprisingly, this worked Indonesia's generals into a frenzy. So great was their concern, they reportedly mulled a plan to sink the Portuguese corvette were it to leave Darwin with Winspeare on board. This was soon rejected due to its ramifications, but a variation on this theme called for sinking the corvette before the UN delegation boarded. Yet another plan called for Jakarta to publish unconfirmed—and unsubstantiated—reports that Indonesian communists were fighting alongside Falintil, this in an attempt to solidify Western support.[23]

Then there were the lingering problems of Com and Suai. With Winspeare apparently leaning toward use of a Portuguese corvette, the generals noted that both these locales were on the coast and easily accessible by ship. They also noted that Suai and Los Palos (adjacent to Com) had airstrips, which could potentially be used by Winspeare in the event he returned to the option of chartering a plane.

Of the two sites, the generals became fixated on Suai. Their military intelligence had gotten wind that Nicolau Lobato and other Fretilin leaders were hunkered down in the central highlands near the town of Maubisse. Though the distance between Maubisse and Suai was a hike of several days in the best of conditions, the Kogasgab planners made the connection and thus convinced themselves that Suai was a likely destination for the UN fact-finders. Deeming it the highest priority to seize both Suai and Los Palos, Kogasgab on the morning of 31 January cut orders for another pair of airborne assaults.[24]

---

21 Airborne Battalion 330 occupied Viqueque, while Infantry Battalion 327 took Betano and headed for Same. Infantry Battalion 327 was able to fully occupy Same as of 3 February. *Ibid.*, pp. 15-16.
22 FBIS, Asia and Pacific edition, 28 January 1976, p. N2; 29 January 1976, p. M1.
23 "The Timor Papers," p. 34. In classified Indonesian military documents written at the time, the possibility was raised that Indonesian communists could be aiding Falintil but no proof had been uncovered. *Laporan Operasi Seroja*, p. 25
24 Subagyo, p. 45.

CHAPTER FOUR

MAKING THE CUT

Brigadier General Yogie Suardi Memet, the Kopassandha commander since May 1975, was a stickler for appearances. From a razor thin moustache, to spit-shined boots, to immaculately pressed uniforms, he came across as more British than Indonesian. There were even rumors, almost certainly true, that he would routinely halt his vehicle just short of the army headquarters in order to wipe down the wheels and give the rubber a perfect ebony sheen before entering.

This contrasted sharply with Yogie's hardscrabble background, where he had risen through the rough and tumble ranks of the paratroopers. As an airborne battalion commander in 1965, he and his men won accolades after tracking down and killing rebel leader Kahar Muzzakar in Sulawesi. He had then served as chief-of-staff for an airborne brigade, followed by a term as commander of an infantry brigade. And understudying for the previous two years as the Kopassandha deputy commander (despite never attending the commando course himself), he was well versed in the corps and its abilities.

But more than that, Yogie had the trust of President Suharto. Following a short-lived challenge to his rule in 1974 during the so-called Malari Affair, Suharto had weeded out several potential competitors from among the top brass. Not only was Yogie untainted by Malari, but he was an ethnic Sundanese from West Java. While exceptions existed, as a general rule there was a glass ceiling at the top of the Indonesian army confounding those who were not ethnic Javanese. Because he was of the wrong pedigree, Yogie was not seen as a threat to power and thus had cemented the president's favor.[1]

---

1   Interview with Atmadji Sumarkidjo, 22 July 2016.

Entrusted as Kopassandha commander, Yogie from the start of his tenure was consumed by the unfolding East Timor insurgency. His commandos has been operating along the 200-kilometer border while the conflict was just below boil during most of 1975, then they had been key components for the airborne assaults when Seroja kicked off in December. Continuing in the nanggala series, Nanggala 6—consisting of a para-commando company from Group 2—had been dispatched to Dili in late December to act as a mobile reserve.

These deployments had not been without issue. Increasingly the commandos grumbled at being misused as light infantry in plodding ground advances, a role for which they were too lightly equipped and which could just as easily have been handled by conventional units.

Worse, there were problems tied to command and control. While Kogasgab was penning the grand strategy in East Timor, there had often been confusion at the tactical level. During the initial Dili parachute drop, for example, hours had passed before Kopassandha commandos and the airborne infantry sorted out their respective chains of command—a time lag that left open an escape route for Falintil to pack up the main *Tropas* armory and disappear into the island's interior with minimum casualties. There had also been incidents of friendly fire between paratroopers and marines landing on the Dili beach, again pointing to inadequate inter-service coordination.

So when it was decided by Kogasgab early on 31 January that the runways at Suai and Los Palos needed to be quickly seized in order to deny them to the UN fact-finding team, Yogie was adamant: he wanted Kopassandha to handle one of the targets alone to both showcase their skills and avoid further command and control confusion. The army chief-of-staff granted him the request, agreeing to a division of labor whereby Kopassandha would tackle Suai, while airborne infantry would handle Los Palos. By noon that same day, Yogie cut orders for the formation of Nanggala 8 to plan and execute an airborne operation into Suai in order to gain control of its runway.[2] The catch: they had to deploy within three days.

There were numerous challenges inherent in this task. First, given the gravity of the assignment and the fact that Kopassandha's reputation was on the line, Yogie wanted to ensure that Nanggala 8 was sufficiently large. The seizure of a runway was a classic para-commando mission for which Groups 1 and 2 were trained and equipped. But stretched by recent and ongoing deployments to Timor, the only fresh para-commandos readily available was

---

2   Nanggala 7, consisting of an augmented *prayudha*, was sent to West Kalimantan in early January 1976.

one 101-man company from Group 2.

To augment that amount, the Kopassandha headquarters turned to Group 4. While more lightly equipped and oriented toward unconventional warfare, Group 4 was tapped for two 72-man *karsa yudha*. Between these and the para-commando company, Nanggala 8 would total almost 250 men.[3]

Due to the urgency of the mission, there was no time to build dioramas of Suai nor even conduct dress rehearsals. As half of Nanggala 8 was drawn from Cijantung and the other half from Magelang, Yogie sought to avoid coordination problems by adding a small staff to oversee both halves. Chosen as commander was Major Soekiman, a short, soft-spoken officer from the Military Academy's Class of 1964. Soekiman had served exclusively with the para-commandos, including a stint as company commander for Group 3 in Solo, then shifting to Group 2 at its intelligence officer.[4]

Rounding out Soekiman's staff was Captain Warow Sende from the academy's Class of 1966 as deputy commander, Captain Johannes Moeryono from the Class of 1967 as intelligence officer, and Captain Sutanto from the Class of 1968 as operations officer. Warow was from Group 4, the other two from Group 2.

Among this staff, perhaps the hardest pressed was intelligence officer Moeryono. This was because Kopassandha was provided with almost no intelligence on Suai. The general geographic picture was well enough known: Suai was the district capital of Cova Lima district, located some 138 kilometers southwest of Dili. To the west of Cova Lima was the border with Indonesia, to the east was Ainaro district, to the north was Bobonaro district, and to the south was the Timor Sea. This particular stretch of Timor's southern coast was parched, with thorny scrub and savannah cut by river deltas and the occasional mangrove swamp. But beyond that description, Kopassandha did not have access to a more detailed cartographic treatment of the district, much less aerial photography.

Largely unknown, too, was the weather. While Timor had a rainy season that ran from December to April, this was more applicable to the mountainous interior. Along the southern coast, Kogasgab could only say that the weather was "variable," which is to say they had no clue.

Truth be told, Suai was not exactly a mystery for Kopassandha. Back in September 1975 during the aggressive expansion of Operation Flamboyan,

---

3   While Nanggala 8 was slightly smaller than Nanggala 5's 263 men, all of the former were destined to jump in what was the largest airborne operation in Kopassandha history.

4   Soekiman served in Group 3 when it still had a para-commando orientation; it had since been transformed into a *sandi yudha* group.

one *prayudha* and one para-commando platoon had been assigned to raid the town. Led by a couple of companies of UDT and Apodeti partisans, they had marched through elephant grass and dried river beds for two days before reaching the district capital. When they tried to destroy a cluster of concrete government buildings, however, their rocket-propelled grenades bounced off and left only superficial damage. Worse, a fierce reaction from resident Falintil defenders sent them sprinting back to the border with casualties. One wounded commando was left behind; he was subsequently executed by Falintil.

Now four months hence, Kogasgab still had no firm grasp over the size and composition of the Falintil presence around Suai. While short on specifics, one of their intelligence estimates suggested Falintil might be operating in company- and platoon-strength across Cova Lima, possibly with access to weapons up to and including rocket launchers, 81mm mortars, and 75mm howitzers.[5]

Obviously, having the 250 men of Nanggala 8 parachute into the midst of all this was hardly an ideal predicament. Fortunately for them, Kogasgab did not intend for the commandos to remain alone for long. On 31 January, at the same time Kopassandha received its orders to assemble Nanggala 8, another order had been issued for an infantry column to march overland from the border to link up with Kopassandha on the Suai runway.

Getting this assignment was Infantry Brigade 2, which had been having its own set of troubles for the past four months. In mid-October 1975, only one of its three organic battalions had reached the border of Portuguese Timor when it was tasked with seizing a trio of border towns held by Fretilin. They seized one objective, but came up short on the other two. One month later, the brigade had reached full strength but still could make little headway against the town of Bobonaro. Not until the end of January 1976, with the help of artillery, armor, and a fourth infantry battalion, did the brigade finally muscle its way into its third and final target.

Not that they had time to celebrate. At 1400 on 31 January, Colonel Mohammad Sanif choppered into Bobonaro. Sanif, a veteran of the airborne battalions, had been serving as the chief-of-staff for the military region covering the Maluku Islands when he was beckoned to Jakarta to join the Kogasgab staff at its inception. With Kogasgab operations loosely divided into those by ground and those by air, Sanif was given the sizable role of overseeing ground combat forces.[6]

---

5   *Laporan Operasi Seroja*, pp. 23-25.
6   Interview with Mohammad Sanif, 16 August 2005.

Gathering with Infantry Brigade 2's staff, Sanif ordered them to send a column south to the Suai runway. The distance was 32 kilometers as the crow flies, but more than 40 kilometers along meandering jungle trails. They were to get there in no less than three days, instructed Sanif, just in time to rendezvous with Nanggala 8.

Factoring in the need to hold their recently conquered real estate around Bobonaro, the brigade could only spare a single battalion for the Suai assignment. Augmented by a pair of rifle companies, one platoon of 80mm mortars, and a second platoon of 120mm mortars, this mini-task force was call-signed *Sikatan* (Indonesian for "Flycatcher"). At 1800 hours on 31 January, just four hours after Sanif's briefing, they began their march out of Bobonaro toward Suai. Joining them were several horses—formerly used by the *Tropas* cavalry group at Bobonaro—to help haul the mortar tubes and baseplates.[7]

For good measure, Kogasgab also passed a request for a platoon of UDT partisans to begin movement toward Suai. This platoon was led by Rui Lopes, the son of a wealthy mestizo family with a once flourishing horse farm near Suai. Rui himself had once been a corporal in the *Tropas* cavalry group. Between the partisans and the Sikatan column, Nanggala 8 would theoretically have a better chance of withstanding what was likely to be a spirited Falintil defense.

*

At just 26 years old, First Lieutenant Muchdi Purwoprandjono was already a seasoned veteran. A member of the Military Academy's Class of 1970, he volunteered and was accepted into the Kopassandha training center at Batu Jajar, West Java, for the commando and airborne courses. Graduating at the start of December 1972, he, like all fresh Batu Jajar graduates, was initially assigned to one of the para-commando groups. And like all other Batu Jajar graduates, he was told he first needed to clock a year of combat experience.

At that time, the only in-country conflict of note was taking place in West Kalimantan. Prior to the change of governments in 1965, Indonesia had waged a poorly-conceived insurgency from Kalimantan into the northern half of the island held by Malaysia and defended by the Commonwealth. After the change in governments, however, Suharto had sought to mend fences with Malaysia and abruptly ceased Indonesia's military adventurism.

Such a fundamental policy shift resulted in a notable scapegoat. For years the Indonesian military had provided arms and training to leftist ethnic Chinese

---

7   *Laporan Operasi Seroja*, p. 41.

guerrillas in West Kalimantan, who had duly conducted raids into Malaysia on Jakarta's behalf. But when the Suharto regime pragmatically redirected their geopolitical orientation toward the right, these armed Chinese remained unapologetically wedded to communism. Moreover, seeing how Suharto was cracking down on leftists across the rest of the country, they defied requests to turn in their weapons.

Incensed at being rebuffed, the Indonesian Armed Forces in the late 1960s began pouring assets into West Kalimantan to wipe out their erstwhile Chinese proxies. By 1972, Kopassandha was being tapped to rotate a task force into the province to spearhead counter-insurgency efforts. On 5 December, the date Muchdi departed for the front line, the Kopassandha unit in West Kalimantan was call-signed Task Force 42. This took its name from the composition of its members: half came from the unconventional warriors at Group 4, and the other half from the para-commandos of Group 2.

Arriving in West Kalimantan, Muchdi barely had time to get his bearings. Just one day after landing, he and three other junior Kopassandha officers were handed parachutes, loaded into a C-47, and dropped into a small government outpost near the Malaysian border. Though the site was already held by an infantry unit, the show-of-force jump was sufficient to earn them a red combat star atop their airborne wings.

Over the ensuing year, Muchdi had his baptism by fire while serving as a para-commando platoon commander in Task Force 42. Their counter-insurgency strategy was dubbed "plowing the fields before planting," and it involved the commandos working their way through the dense jungle and crocodile-infested swamps in extended lines parallel to the Malaysian border. In this way, they tried to slowly flush out the ethnic Chinese guerrillas.[8]

By the opening of 1974, Muchdi was back at Group 2 in Magelang and a year after that he was promoted to company commander. This gave him control over 101 para-commandos broken into a headquarters staff and three 30-man platoons. Each of the platoons, in turn, was divided into a command staff and three 8-man squads.

When the call came on 31 January 1976 for his company to join Nanggala 8, Muchdi had been their leader for half a year. Over the course of the next two days, he and his men busied themselves sorting through gear. Although Kopassandha had been transitioning to the U.S.-made M16A1 as their primary assault rifle, the decision was made for all Timor-bound nanggala teams to use the Soviet AK-47. Kopassandha had used the AK-47 for most of the previous

---

8   Interview with Muchdi Purwoprandjono, 27 April 2016.

decade, and the reason to go back to this rifle was twofold. First, despite its heavier weight compared to the M16A1, the AK-47 was demonstrably more durable and reliable. This counted for much in rugged tropical environments.

Second, Kopassandha was continuing with the weak fiction that the Indonesians fighting in Timor were volunteers rather than formal Indonesian military units—which theoretically did not make them privy to U.S. weapons. But Kogasgab had hardly been enforcing this cover story among all Seroja participants: when Nanggala 5 jumped into Dili, for instance, the Kopassandha commandos used the AK-47, but subsequent waves of airborne infantry were carrying the M16A1.

For heavier weapons, Muchdi's para-commandos carried a hodgepodge of weapons from across the geopolitical spectrum. This was because Indonesia had been weaving a non-aligned path, or at least paying lip service to one, for much of its history. As a result, its armed forces had accepted military aid of varying quality from the East, West, and in between.

For its squad automatic weapon, Group 2 had the RPD light machine gun gifted from the Soviet Union in the early 1960s. It chambered the same 7.62 x 39mm cartridge as the AK-47, which eased logistical requirements for Nanggala 8. Every squad in Muchdi's company carried one RPD.

For a bigger punch, Group 2 was outfitted with the M57 grenade launcher. Though superficially similar to the Soviet RPG-2 rocket-propelled grenade, the M57 had cut its own evolutionary path as Yugoslavia's attempt to improve on Germany's World War Two-era Panzerfaust. Its 90mm warhead was larger than the RPG-2, and it employed a counter-mass system (blowing a packet of sand out the rear) in an attempt to extend its range out to 200 meters. These had been supplied by Belgrade in the early 1960s and every squad in Group 2 had one, though it was an unpopular item with the commandos because of its excessive weight.

For longer ranges, Group 2 wielded the hand-held 50mm mortar. These were made in Indonesia's own Pindad weapons factory based on a Yugoslavian design. Weighing almost 5.5 kilos, they could lob rounds out to a maximum 460 meters. Every platoon in Group 2 had one of these tubes.

By the evening of 2 February, Muchdi's company had all their weapons and equipment sorted and packed. The next day they would be heading to war.

*

Surrounded by acres of banana and rubber trees, the Kopassandha complex in Cijantung was an oasis of order and discipline. From manicured lawns, to white-washed rocks along roadside, to the vaguely colonial lines of its headquarters building, it radiated military efficiency. This extended to the satellite compounds of low-slung barracks and storerooms to its immediate west and northwest, the homes to Group 1 and Group 4.

To ease with administration, General Yogie had handed the bulk of Timor assignments to these two groups over the past year. And when the order came to form Nanggala 8, it was Group 4 that again got the nod to contribute two 72-man *karsa yudha*.

One of these was Karysa Yudha 82 led by Captain Sudiyono. A member of the Class of 1967, Sudiyono had been popular among his peers for his affable personality. His deputy was Captain Dolfi Rondonuwu, a graduate of the Class of 1968. Shortly after getting his commando qualification, Dolfi had apprenticed in Group 1 and was posted to the logistics staff with the task force fighting in West Kalimantan. Under his watch, there had been an unfortunate incident whereby an overladen landing craft capsized while approaching the riverbank; his fellow commandos had not let him live down the fact he lost his AK-47 in the sunken vessel.

After West Kalimantan, Dolfi had transferred to Group 4. Like their U.S. Green Beret counterparts, who had insisted their members be fluent in at least one foreign tongue, Group 4 at the time was toying with a secondary language requirement for all its members. One *prayudha*, for example, was learning English; another, Arabic. Dolfi was in the *prayudha* learning Mandarin Chinese, preparing themselves for behind-the-line action in the event of being overrun by China.[9]

Before reaching any level of linguistic fluency, Dolfi at the start of 1975 was sent to the Timor border for Operation Flamboyan. He then spent most of the year training partisans, conducting intelligence forays and, near the end of their deployment, staging an ill-fated raid on the border town of Atabae that resulted in the loss of two commandos. Dolfi was now getting ready to clock his second Timor deployment in as many years.

Under Karsa Yudha 82 was a headquarters element of 24 men and four 12-man *prayudha*. Two *prayudha* were led by Lieutenants Suwarto and Damung, both of whom were veteran sergeants who had converted to officer status. The other two were led by Lieutenant Eduardus Simbolon, a member of the Class of 1970, and Lieutenant Hakim Saleh Umpusinga, a signals officer from the Class of 1971.

---

9   Interview with Dolfi Rondonuwu, 25 May 1999.

The second *karsa yudha* assigned to Nanggala 8 was Karya Yudha 81. This was led by Captain A.M. Hendropriyono, a member of the Class of 1967. As he was still two weeks shy of completing an infantry officer training course in Bandung, the 72-man unit was temporarily led by his deputy, Captain Heri Tabri from the Class of 1968. The two had a close working relationship, abetted by the fact that Heri was engaged to marry the younger sister of Hendropriyono's wife.

Of the four *prayudha* in Karsa Yudha 81, the first was led by Captain Suparmin, a former sergeant that was almost a generation older than his peers. The other three were led by young Military Academy graduates: Alberto Nainggolan from the Class of 1970; Subagyo Hadi Siswoyo, also from the Class of 1970; and Fathomi, a signals officer from the Class of 1971.

As a *prayudha* commander, 29-year old First Lieutenant Subagyo Hadi Siswoyo was new to the job. That is not to say he was without combat experience. Along with Muchdi, the Group 2 company commander assigned to Nanggala 8, Subagyo had completed commando training in December 1972 and then headed to West Kalimantan for a year of counter-insurgency sweeps.

Returning to Java, Subagyo had received additional *sandi yudha* instruction while posted to Group 3 in Solo. In mid-1975, he took leave of Solo to attend a three-month intelligence course at Bogor. He had not arrived at his current assignment with Group 4 until near year's end.[10]

On 1 February 1976, Subagyo and the rest of the officers from Karsa Yudha 81 and 82 were beckoned to the Kopassandha headquarters building. General Yogie himself gave the briefing, telling them only that they were required to parachute into Suai in three days in order to block a possible visit by a UN delegation. The general offered them few other details, as he himself knew little more. It was readily apparent to Subagyo and his fellow officers that plans seemed disturbingly rushed.[11]

Returning to their barracks, the two *karsa yudha* began to prepare equipment. Just as with the Group 2 contingent, they were informed that they would be using the reliable AK-47 as their assault rifle. A sufficient number were retrieved from the armory, with folding stock models given to officers and wooden stock versions given to other ranks. All of the men managed to find time over the following day to get to the range to calibrate sights and re-familiarize themselves with the AK-47's idiosyncrasies.

Unlike the para-commandos of Group 2, the special warfare troops of

---

10 Interview with Subagyo H.S., 17 May 2016.
11 Subagyo, p. 49.

Group 4 relied on guile rather than violence of action. As such, they did not normally carry any weapons heavier than their assault rifle and grenades. They would not be taking any machine guns, rocket launchers, or hand-held mortars. Were they to stage any frontal assaults against a well-entrenched adversary, they would be at a distinct disadvantage.

On the afternoon of 2 February, the men began packing their RI T-10 parachutes and reserves. The RI T-10 was an Indonesian clone of the venerable T-10, the result of an effort the previous decade to bust American sanctions against the sale of military equipment to the Sukarno regime. It was slightly reduced in diameter from the American original, along with modified toggles and the addition of two gores on each side of the canopy to theoretically add maneuverability. This remained little more than theory, however, as the RI T-10 was in every practical sense a non-steerable parachute system lacking any appreciable maneuverability.[12]

Packing his chute, Subagyo recalled that he had used the RI T-10 on a combat mission in December 1972 when he had jumped—along with Muchdi—into the border outpost in West Kalimantan. On that occasion, they had landed in daylight at a quiet drop-zone already secured by fellow Indonesian infantrymen.

This time around, he strongly suspected, the reception would not be as cordial.

---

12 Interview with Erlangga Suryadarma, 7 June 2006.

CHAPTER FIVE
RECON

On the evening of 1 February, Vittorio Winspeare and his team were wheels up in Jakarta and inbound for Australia. He had been telegraphing the move for days, all the while challenging Fretilin, the Portuguese, the Indonesians, and Australians to make some headway in logistical arrangements for his intended visit to the Timor countryside.

Much of the ensuing talk had been chicken-or-the-egg circular argumentation. The Portuguese agreed to have one of their vessels transport Winspeare to the Timor coast—but only if Indonesia provided a security guarantee. In response, Indonesian Foreign Minister Malik on 30 January claimed Jakarta had no problem with a visit, provided—he ominously added—Winspeare was "willing to take the risk." [1]

Complicating matters, most of Winspeare's options for a landing site were fast wafting away. Malik correctly claimed on 30 January that pro-Indonesian forces were already occupying Viqueque. He also claimed they were mopping up in Same and fighting was underway in Suai. He was slightly premature on the second claim and bluffing on the third, though the UN team would have been hard pressed to independently corroborate any of this.

While short of any breakthrough, Winspeare reiterated he was ready to take up the Portuguese offer to use their corvette. In addition, Portugal approved use of their corvette's radio for contacting Fretilin pockets inside Timor; Jose Ramos-Horta had already flown ahead to Australia to assist with coordination.[2]

---

1 FBIS, Asia and Pacific edition, 3 February 1976, p. M1.
2 "The Timor Papers," p. 34.

By the time he landed in Darwin on the morning of 2 February, Winspeare wasted no time linking up with Ramos-Horta and Tony Belo, the Fretilin radioman.[3] Over the course of their conversation, Ramos-Horta insisted that Same was a viable meeting site—this despite Malik's claim about mopping up in that town, as well as Fretilin's own earlier statements that nearby Betano was being besieged by Indonesian forces.

Next, Winspeare headed for the Darwin wharf. Tied up alongside was the pride of the Portuguese fleet, the *João Roby*. One of four new *Baptista de Andrade* class corvettes, it was designed at the start of the decade to project strength to the ends of Portugal's far-flung empire. Reality, however, proved to be far different. After an emergency request from the besieged Timor colonial government in September 1975, the first of these formidable corvettes, the *Afonso Cerqueira*, arrived in the waters off Atauro during the first week of October. A little over a month later, on 23 November, it was joined by the *João Roby*. Both warships were sitting off the coast of Atauro during early December, their radars clearly picking up the formation of Indonesian C-130 transports that approached Dili and disgorged paratroopers.

Lethal yet impotent, the two corvettes then loaded aboard the residual Portuguese colonial presence and set sail for Darwin.[4] The *João Roby* was still there on 2 February when Winspeare and his deputy Erik Jensen approached. Recalled Jensen:

> I remember it well because we were piped on board—the only time I have had that experience. After talking things over with the commanding officer, a charming young man seemingly unaffected by regime change in Lisbon, we were served ultra-dry white wine and salt cod in the best Portuguese naval tradition.[5]

Over the course of their meal the Portuguese repeated their offer to transport the UN team to waters off Timor, then let them take a skiff to shore. It was roughly 700 kilometers from Darwin to the southern Timor coast. As the *João Roby* could maintain a speed of 24 knots, the journey there would take about 16 hours.

The Portuguese also noted that their warship had a helipad. If the UN could borrow a helicopter, they could stage from the *João Roby* by rotary-wing once they neared Timor.[6]

---

3   FBIS, Asia and Pacific edition, 3 February 1976, p. M1.
4   On 20 January, the corvette *Oliveira e Carmo* arrived at Darwin, allowed the *Afonso Cerqueira* to depart for Europe the following week. FBIS, Asia and Pacific edition, 22 January 1976, p. M1.
5   Correspondence with Erik Jensen, 14 January 2017.
6   Way, p. 689.

None of these were optimal solutions. Jensen was particularly somber, noting that Fretilin might suggest a location they knowingly did not control, thus enabling them to point the finger at Indonesia for sabotaging the visit. And if they tried to keep their landing site a secret—which Winspeare had earlier hinted was his preference—they risked accidental bombardment by pro-Indonesia forces.[7]

Shortly after the UN envoys departed the *João Roby*, Ramos-Horta and Belo arrived at the wharf. Taking up the Portuguese radio offer, they were steered to the communications room to use its transmitter to contact their Fretilin comrades inside Timor.

The next morning, 3 February, Winspeare met Ramos-Horta for the second time in as many days. However, the Fretilin spokesman still offered no new information on a possible meeting site. Moreover, the pro-Indonesia PGET proxy government had just issued a threat to shoot down or sink any aircraft or vessel approaching the Timorese coast; they further added that they did not wish to assume responsibility for the safety of the UN delegation. The PGET proclamation lent Indonesia plausible deniability, but it was clear that Jakarta was not in an accommodating mood.[8]

His patience wearing thin, Winspeare gave Ramos-Horta an ultimatum. If Fretilin could not come up with a meeting site quickly, he expected written notice from Ramos-Horta stating as much. Dejected, the Fretilin representative said he would prepare something.[9]

By the late afternoon of 3 February, Winspeare's normally adequate reservoir of diplomatic etiquette had drained. Instead of Ramos-Horta penning him the requested note about his failure to confirm a landing site, the Fretilin representative had instead sent a letter to the UN Security Council complaining about a lack of cooperation from the Australians and Indonesians. In it, he claimed that he tried to communicate with Fretilin inside Timor on the corvette's radio, but the wavelength had been jammed with profanities in Portuguese, Indonesian, and the Timorese language of Tetum.

Meeting with an Australian diplomat that evening, Winspeare had had enough of waiting and excuses. "I came to Darwin to listen to maniacs," he lamented.[10]

*

---

7   Way, p. 686.
8   FBIS, Asia and Pacific edition, 4 February 1976, p. Q1.
9   Way, p. 688.
10 *Ibid.*

As 3 February dawned on Java, the Group 2 headquarters at Magelang was a buzz of activity. Weapons, ammunition, and parachutes had been loaded into a convoy of trucks, in front of which stood a company of para-commandos at parade rest.

Lieutenant Muchdi, the company commander, requested a final headcount before mounting the vehicles. Exactly 100 officers and other ranks were accounted for, he was told. That left one missing.

"Corporal Sudiman is in the brig," one of the sergeants reminded Muchdi. Sudiman was a good trooper and had earlier served as Muchdi's adjutant, but he was languishing in a cell after returning from an unauthorized three-month absence.

Muchdi offered an instant pardon and ordered Sudiman to be released. He wanted to go to Timor with a full contingent of 101 commandos.[11]

Piling aboard the trucks, they made the 44 kilometer journey to the Jogjakarta airport without incident. Waiting for them were two F28 jetliners operated by state-owned airline Garuda Indonesia. The F28 was a short-range jet with sixty-five seats produced by the Dutch aircraft manufacturer Fokker. To support the Seroja operation, Garuda Indonesia had been required to allocate fifteen F28s, plus another six of its turboprop F27 airliners. They came with their normal compliment of Garuda pilots and stewardesses, leading to the somewhat surreal situation of the battle-ready commandos getting served peanuts and soft drinks by petite attendants as they were whisked to Bali.

Once in Bali, the para-commando company crossed the tarmac to a pair of Indonesian Air Force C-130 transports for the flight to Kupang. While the C-130 was theoretically its fixed-wing workhorse, the air force had been caught ill-prepared when Seroja first took shape. Of the eleven airframes in their inventory, only one was deemed airworthy because they had been tardy in replenishing stocks of specialized lubricants. Scouring the markets in Hong Kong and Singapore during November, they rushed in sixteen tons of oil and were able to get nine planes operable for the first airborne drop in Dili. As several aircraft were undergoing maintenance and repairs after the hectic first month of Seroja, six were still available as of the end of January 1976.[12]

By the time the para-commandos landed in Kupang, it was shortly after noon and the oppressive heat was shimmering off the Penfui runway. Disembarking, the troops scrambled to find shade under a row of tents erected along one side of the strip.

---

11   Muchdi interview.
12   Interview with Saleh Basarah, 6 June 2006.

CHAPTER FIVE - RECON

The tents had actually been set up the previous day for Airborne Battalion 502. That battalion had participated in the Dili jump two months earlier; along with its sister battalion, Airborne Battalion 501, it had seen heavy action during the opening act of Seroja. The decision had then been made to withdraw them back to Java for refitting, and the 502nd had already boarded a navy ship at Dili for the journey to Surabaya.

Before they had reached their destination, the seizure of Suai and Los Palos suddenly became top priorities. At General Yogie's insistence, Kopassandha was given the task of jumping into Suai on its own. In a division of labor, the airborne infantry would alone tackle Los Palos. Instead of rest and refitting, the 502nd diverted to Kupang and was told they would be doing the jump.

Earlier that morning, the 502nd had packed aboard six C-130s and jumped into Los Palos. Falintil had been cooperative this time around, fading into the jungle and letting the paratroopers consolidate their hold against virtually no opposition.[13]

Nanggala 8 should have it so lucky. While his men caught a brief rest, Lieutenant Muchdi was directed to the apron. There the senior staff of Nanggala 8—Major Soekiman, operations officer Sutanto, and intelligence officer Moeryono—were awaiting him near a West German-made Bolkow Bo-105 chopper. This was operated by Pelita Air Service, an aviation subsidiary of the state-owned Pertamina oil company. Like Garuda, Pelita had been pressed into contributing a large number of fixed-wing and rotary-wing assets to assist the Seroja campaign, including two Bolkows.[14]

Because Kogasgab had yet to provide aerial photographs of any clarity, the decision had been made to fly a reconnaissance mission over Suai in order to select a drop-zone. The four Kopassandha officers climbed into the rear of the Bolkow and were airborne by 1500 hours, providing just enough time to get to Suai and back before sunset.

En route to their target, the Bolkow pilot was instructed to remain at a relatively high altitude. This was because Falintil had dramatically demonstrated during the Dili drop that its assortment of machine guns and assault rifles were more than up to the task of hitting low-flying aircraft. But the high altitude also meant the four Bolkow passengers could see little apart from tree canopies and, briefly in the distance, Suai's 900-meter grass runway.

---

13 Subroto, p. 184. While Airborne Battalion 502 jumped onto the Los Palos runway, Infantry Battalion 312 was simultaneously landed by naval ship at the adjacent town of Lautem. *Laporan Pelaksanaan Tugas Operasi Kogasgab "S,"* p. 15.

14 Pelita Air Services supported Kogasgab with two F28 jetliners, two F27 turboprops, one BAC 1-11 short-range jetliner, and two Bolkow choppers. *Ibid.*, p. 12.

By the time they returned to Penfui, the sun was edging below the horizon. On the tarmac were four Garuda F28s, which had flown directly from Jakarta's Halim Perdanakusuma airport with the two *karsa yudha* from Group 4.

With all of Nanggala 8 now present, its officers were ordered to the terminal building for a briefing. Also there was Colonel Sanif, the Kogasgab ground forces commander, as well as several representatives from military intelligence. As the ranking officer, Sanif presided over the meeting. He listened attentively to the findings from the Bolkow reconnaissance flight, then consulted with the available maps of the vicinity. This produced a lot of feet shuffling, as the recon had produced next to no information of value and the maps were little more than Xeroxes of a rudimentary Portuguese chart produced a decade earlier. What they could deduce was that the airstrip was in a north-south orientation about 2 kilometers inland from the beach. The town of Suai was located to the south/southwest of the runway, the distance between which was around 3 kilometers.

Shrugging his shoulders, Sanif gestured toward the map. The drop-zone would be the 2 kilometer stretch between the southern end of the runway and the beach, he decreed. Upon landing, the members of Nanggala 8 would only have to follow their compasses north to reach the airfield.[15]

Sanif saved the bad news for last, of which there was plenty. Years of attrition had taken a heavy toll on the offensive capability of the Indonesian Air Force: all of its Soviet-made bombers and fighters were grounded from a lack of spare-parts, as were its World War Two-era P-51 Mustangs and B-25 Mitchells. Kogasgab had been allocated just one vintage B-26 light bomber and one AC-47, a gunship version of the aging C-47 transport. But as it was deemed too dangerous to use them in close proximity to troops during the early morning hours, no air support sorties were scheduled.[16]

Though naval gunfire had assisted during the assaults on Dili and Betano, this, too, was unavailable.

Just as bad, the Sikatan task force from Brigade 2, which was supposed to rendezvous with Nanggala 8 at the runway, was having problems of its own. After marching out of Bobonaro on the night of 31 January, they had covered 4 kilometers to the village of Tapo at a brisk pace. After that, they got bogged down on the 10-kilometer stretch to the Holpolec trail junction. They were still there on 2 February, claiming—probably with some hyperbole—that they

---

15 Subagyo H.S. interview.
16 Basarah interview. During the Los Palos jump at 0900 on 3 February, one B-26 had conducted bombing runs.

were confronted by up to six Falintil companies.[17]

As of the evening of 3 February, Sikatan had just passed the village of Lolotoi and were on a southeast heading. But they still had another 15 kilometers to go before reaching the coastal road parallel to the beach, then a trek of another 10 kilometers west toward Suai. They would be late for their rendezvous by at least a day.

The UDT partisans, too, were behind schedule and there was no good estimate on when they would arrive.

As for the estimated Falintil size around Suai, Sanif still had no updates. But as they assumed the entire local populous would be hostile, Sanif was not optimistic. Casualties for Nanggala 8, he calculated, would hit 50 percent.

Major Soekiman, the Nanggala 8 commander, was not the most forceful personality in Kopassandha. But even he began to grow animated and register reservations about the lack of preparedness.

Company commander Muchdi was equally troubled. Bemoaned Muchdi in hindsight, "Everything was wrong for an airborne operation."[18]

*

At 1900, the other ranks of Nanggala 8 gathered around Penfui's dilapidated hanger for a final briefing. Presiding over this was Colonel Johnny Sinaga, an intelligence officer assigned to Kogasgab.[19]

Sinaga basically gave a rehash of what Sanif told the officers. The Falintil presence in Suai was not known with precision, but they would have a hostile reception and could expect 50 percent casualties. Not surprisingly, this did not go down well with the troops.

Copies of the Xeroxed maps had been distributed among the men, which generated a wave of snickers. Their drop-zone was the stretch between the beach and the runway, Sinaga told the commandos. While forested, the tree cover was far less dense than other parts of Indonesia. Though their chutes had minimum maneuverability, and visibility was diminished during the early morning hours, they stood a good chance of reaching the ground without getting strung up in the canopy.

Once on the ground, they were to check their compasses and head north toward the airstrip. Along the way, in the fog of battle, they might encounter

---

17 *Laporan Operasi Seroja*, p. 41.
18 Muchdi interview.
19 Interview with Suwito H.A., 7 June 2016.

fellow commandos or opposing Falintil. To differentiate friend from foe, their password and countersign was based on the Kopassandha headwear: the approaching party would say "*baret*" [beret] and the proper reply would be "*merah*" [red]. Anybody not giving the right reply was to be considered enemy.

The briefing over, the commandos were told to get some rest in their tents. Four C-130 transports were on the far end of the tarmac. They would begin loading at 0300, 4 February.

*

Lieutenant Subagyo opened his eyes at 12 midnight. He had managed to sleep for three hours, nothing short of amazing given the background noise and adrenaline coursing through their collective veins. Strolling to the hanger, he joined several dozen *prayudha* members who were swapping tales and advice. Thanks to the prerequisite for all Kopassandha newcomers to spend time in Kalimantan, every officer had seen at least some combat; nobody would be having their baptism by fire the next day. But all of their experiences paled to that of Captain Suparmin, the grizzled *prayudha* commander who had served as a non-commissioned officer the previous decade during tough campaigns against the Dutch in Papua and Commonwealth in Kalimantan.

Regaling the crowd about his 1962 jump into Papua, Suparmin ended with a wizened tip. "If you see that your main chute has deployed properly," he counseled, "the first thing you do is get rid of your reserve."

The reserve chute was in a large chest pack affixed to the front of the parachute harness with snap hooks. Unsnapping and discarding it in midair was not something taught in airborne school, but Suparmin said it was the smart choice on two counts. First, it would allow for an unobscured view of the ground. Second, it would lighten their weight by 8 kilos—not an insignificant amount for some of the smaller Indonesians.

As Suparmin seemed to speak with authority, Subagyo made a mental note to discard his reserve as suggested.

Talk then shifted to the likelihood of receiving ground fire while still descending in the air. This vulnerability was the fear of all parachutists, and had become a deadly reality during the Dili jump two months earlier. According to standard procedure, their assault rifles were securely fixed under the right shoulder, muzzle facing down and pistol grip to the rear to reduce the chances of entanglement during parachute deployment. The rifle sling was fixed diagonally across the chest and under the parachute harness, eliminating the chance of it slipping off during the jump. Even so, some of the commandos began to talk wistfully about clutching their weapons while in the air and returning fire toward Failintil below.

At 0100, 4 February, Subagyo walked to the apron in front of the parked C-130 transports to make final preparations of his gear. He would be carrying a folding stock AK-47 with two 30-round magazines taped together, one inserted and ready to fire in the rifle's magazine well.

Inside his rucksack, to be secured under his reserve chute, were 750 more bullets, two grenades, and a tin of fried rice. Affixed on his web belt was a commando knife, a pistol with two magazines, and a canteen. Everyone was also given one *nasi bungkus*—a simple rice meal wrapped in banana leaf and waxed paper—that had been prepared by a Padang restaurant near Penfui airbase. These were stuffed into shirt or pants pockets for a quick breakfast right after they parachuted the next morning.[20]

Combined with their parachutes and reserves, this was a heavy load for the officers and men of the two *karsa yudha*. They had it good, however, compared to the para-commando company. Heavier equipped than their colleagues from Group 4, the para-commandos were also hauling cumbersome rocket launchers, extra rockets, mortar tubes, mortar rounds, machine guns, and 80-round drum magazines. Recalled one of the squad commanders, Sergeant Suwito:

> I was carrying 500 bullets, two mortar rounds, and two rockets. I weighed 63 kilos, but my supplies and chutes weighed 70 kilos. It was so heavy I needed help walking.[21]

As Suwito struggled with his load, next to him Corporal Sutisna from the command staff of Karsa Yudha 82 wrestled to secure his bulky parachute harness. A tight grin broke over his face, as if receiving a premonition. "Who knows?" he asked Suwito. "Maybe tomorrow we won't meet again."[22]

*

At 0300, Nanggala 8 began filing aboard the aircraft and took seats. Divided among the first two planes was the para-commando company. The two *karsa yudha* were in the third and fourth planes. It was a cramped fit in all four, close to capacity.

Before he had donned his reserve chute and rucksack, Lieutenant Muchdi

---
20 Subagyo, p. 56.
21 Suwito interview.
22 *Ibid.*

recalled the 50 percent casualty estimate given by Sanif. Depressed at the thought he might lose half his company in a few short hours, he walked through the first two planes to look them over and offer final words of encouragement.

Muchdi paused before Corporal Sudiman, his adjutant who he had sprung from the brig, and gave him a pat on the helmet.

Sudiman, who had yet to marry, looked upward and forced a smile. "Take care of my parents."[23]

Muchdi waved off the grim request. "All will be fine," he answered in a tone that convinced no one.

---

23 Muchdi interview.

Vittorio Winspeare, Director General for the UN Office in Geneva, August 1973.
(*UN photograph*)

Jose Ramos-Horta addressing the UN Security Council, 15 December 1975.
(*UN photograph*)

Major General Benny Moerdani visiting East Timor, circa 1976.

The UN team in Dili confers with a PGET official posing as a naval officer, 20 January 1976. From left to right is Harald Smaage, Gilberto Schlitter-Silva, Erik Jensen, and Vittorio Winspeare. (*courtesy Erik Jensen*)

Lt. Subagyo Hadi Siswoyo and his *prayudha* in Suai, February 1976.

Lieutenants Muchdi Purwoprandjono and Subagyo Hadi Siswoyo in Suai, February 1976.

Captain Hendropriyono (center) and Major Mulyadi (right), commander of Battalion 123, meet with Timorese civilians near Laklubar, mid-1976.
(*courtesy A.M. Hendropriyono*)

```
DEPARTEMEN PERTAHANAN KEAMANAN
KOMANDO DAERAH PERTAHANAN KEAMANAN
            TIMOR TIMUR


                        FORMULIR - BERITA


D A R I      :  PANG KODAHANKAM
U N T U K    :  1. DAN YONIF 123
                2. TEAM SUS
TEMBUSAN     :  1. POS KOPAS
                2. AS-1 S/D 6 KODAHANKAM
                3. DAN RTP 13 KMA 15 KMA DAN 16


KLASIFIKASI  :  RAHASIA
N O M E R    :  TR/    -1/1976  TTK


AAA  TTK     PANG BESERTA STAF DAN SELURUH JAJARAN KODAHANKAN MENG-
             UCAPKAN SELAMAT ATAS HASIL YG TELAH DICAPAI PD OPS TGL
             0923 0500 OLEH YONIF 123 DAN TEAM SUS DBP KAPT INF HEN-
             DRO DI RUDUHAN KPLES (KV 1530) DGN DITEMBAK MATINYA SA-
             LAH SEORANG PIMP GTF BERNAMA LEONARDO COSTA ALVES RA -
             NGEL (DAN SAT RAMAHANA) TTK


BBB  TTK     SEMOGA TUHAN YME MEMBERIKAN LINDUNGAN-NYA KPD KITA SE-
             MUA TTK


CCC  TTK     UMP KMA PANG KHM TTK HBS (X)


                              TGL/WKT PEMBIKINAN : 0929 1030


PENGIRIM :
N A M A         :  DADING KALBUADI
PANGKAT/JAB     :  BRIGJEN TNI/PANG KODAHANKAM
TANDA TANGAN    :
```

Memorandum from Brigadier General Dading Kalbuadi
confirming the death of Ramahana, 29 September 1976.

Hendropriyono (left) and Francisco Osorio Soares (second from right). (*courtesy A.M. Hendropriyono*)

Hendropriyono and Zeka Vong (right). (*courtesy A.M. Hendropriyono*)

Francisco Osorio Soares (left), Hendropriyono,
and Gatot Purwanto (right, foreground). (*courtesy A.M. Hendropriyono*)

Hendropriyono and members of Nanggala 13.
Kneeling second from right is Vidal Sarmento. (*courtesy A.M. Hendropriyono*)

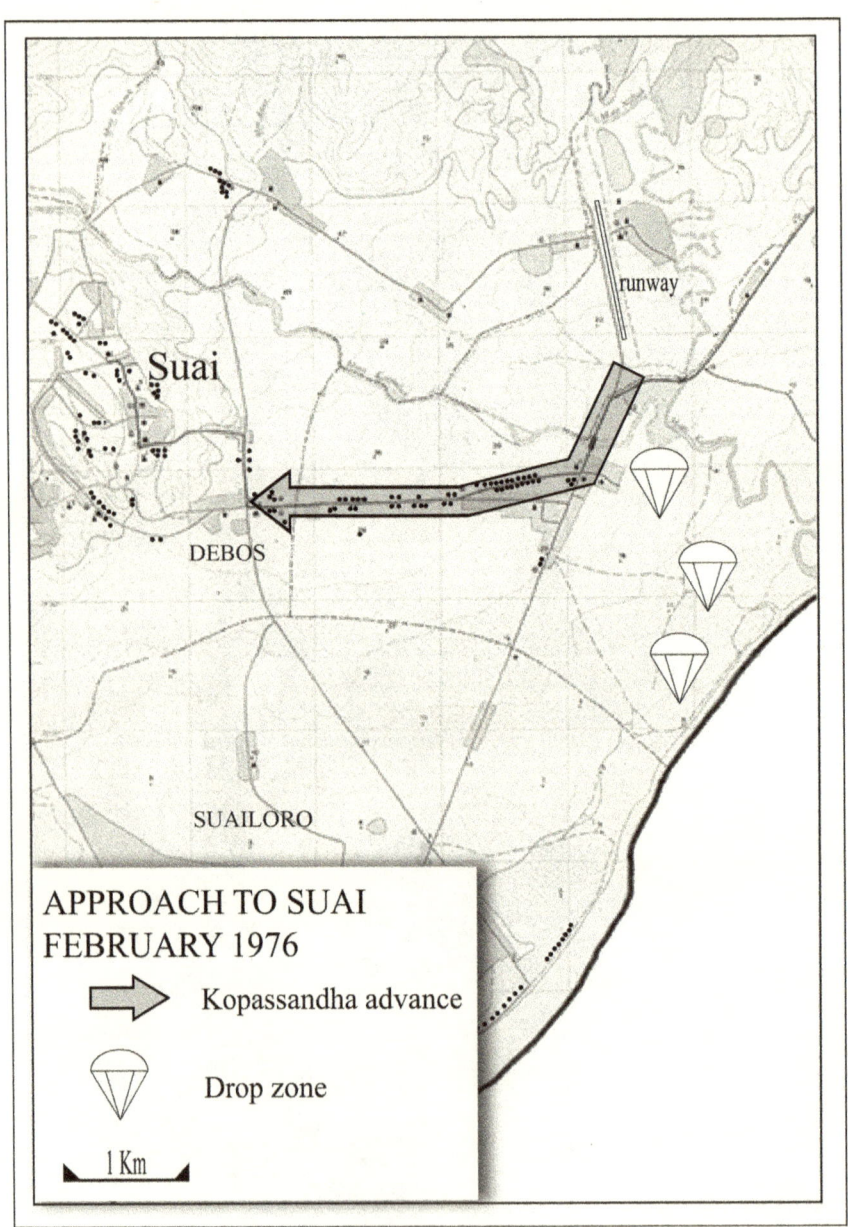

CHAPTER SIX

HELL IN A VERY, VERY SMALL PLACE

Captain Subagyo Saleh stared intently at the red screen of the AN/APN-59 radar. He was navigator in the lead C-130, meaning an immense weight was on his shoulders to correctly steer them to the Suai drop-zone. The challenges were legion: it was dark, Timor was still a new and unfamiliar theater of combat, and there were no additional navigational aids installed on their plane.

Then there was the intimidation factor from the fourth person in the cockpit. Major General Benny Moerdani, the head of military intelligence, was among several officers who had arrived at Kupang at the eleventh hour and boarded the Suai-bound armada as observers. Divided among the other three planes was Colonel Djasmin, the Kopassandha deputy commander, Lt. Colonel Wismoyo Arismunandar, the Kopassandha intelligence officer, and Lt. Colonel Sutedjo, the Kopassandha operations officer.[1]

After waiting an hour on the tarmac with its complement of Nanggala 8 on board, the first C-130 lumbered down the runway at 0400. The lead pilot, Lt. Colonel O.H. Wello, maintained a southwesterly heading as they waited for the other three planes to get airborne and catch up.

Once they were in string formation, Wello made a 180 degree turn and headed northeast. In radio silence, the four planes proceeded parallel to the Timorese coastline off port side.

Forty minutes into the flight, Moerdani began peppering Subagyo with questions. The most frequent: "Where is the drop-zone?"

---

1   Interview with Djasmin, 19 June 1999.

Subagyo did his best to sound confident. But navigating was as much an art as a science, and he was at the limits of his abilities interpreting the terrain features flickering on the plane's aging radar.

"Not yet, Sir."

Every other minute, Moerdani asked the same question. And got the same reply.

Finally at 0455, Subagyo drew close to the radar and saw the faint image of a hook in the shoreline. He was certain it matched the unique shape of the small bay near Suai. Relaying this to Wello, the pilot banked left toward the Timor coast.

Moerdani, who had participated in his own night combat jump in Papua back in 1962, remained inquisitive. "What is the TOP?"

Subagyo struggled to recall the acronym. Then he remembered: *Tinggi Operasi Perterjungan*—Altitude for Dropping. "One thousand feet, Sir."

Their drop altitude had earlier been a subject of discussion. The mainstay of Falintil was the Getme rifle, which could fire out to 500 meters, or more than 1,600 feet. This had put their C-130 fleet over Dili well within range, and the aircraft paid a heavy price. Not only did four of the nine planes received significant bullet damage during that operation, but one loadmaster had been shot dead while standing near a rear paratroop door.

To reduce risk to the planes this time around, the decision had been made for the four Suai aircraft fly at 3,000 feet for most of the flight, then for the lead plane to drop down to 1,000 feet just two minutes before the jump. As soon as their commandos had leapt, Wello would pull back to 3,000 feet to escape from rifle range. Each of the subsequent planes would be 300 feet behind the one in front, and stacked 50 feet higher in altitude to ensure that it would not collide with parachutists from the planes ahead.[2]

At 0500, Wello began the rapid descent to 1,000 feet. Taking this as his cue, Subagyo activated the air deflectors in front of the paratroop doors and sounded the bell in the rear cabin.

*

In the back of the first C-130, a pair of jumpmasters heard the bell and in a bellowing voice ordered the parachutists to stand. They yelled back '*commando*' in unison. As they fastened their static lines, air force loadmasters opened the two side doors. Air rushed in and the sound of the engines increased exponentially.

---

2   Interview with Subagyo Saleh, 18 November 2016.

CHAPTER SIX - HELL IN A VERY, VERY SMALL PLACE

One of the jumpmasters looked out the door and squinted. The eastern sky was only starting to show signs of orange; the view below remained gunmetal gray. Ahead of them, however, there was a lighter line before the gray visibly darkened. He correctly interpreted that as the coastline and jungle beyond it. Waiting until the darker gray hues were below the aircraft, he gave the hand signal to begin jumping.

Among the first in his stick, Sergeant Suwito, the squad commander laden with 70 kilos of gear, was relieved to step into the dawn sky. Swinging under his main chute, he unclipped the reserve and let it tumble away. As the jungle canopy rushed closer, he instinctively covered his face.

Crashing through branches, his head snapped forward as he came to an abrupt halt. Letting his eyes adjust to the darkness, he could see that his chute was snagged in a tree and he was hanging a meter from the ground. This had fortuitously spared his knees and ankles the shock of a hard landing.

Releasing his harness, he dropped to the ground and collected his gear. Six other para-commandos had landed safely nearby.

Remembering the *nasi bungkus* in his pocket, Suwito paused to eat. When he opened the wax paper, however, the stench of rancid food was overpowering. With little choice but to go hungry, he and his six colleagues began their cautious trek north toward the runway.[3]

In the second C-130, the jumpmasters correctly identified the shoreline and signaled the men to start jumping. In less than a minute, all the para-commandos were out the doors. This included company commander Muchdi, who craned his head upward to ensure his main chute was properly deployed. Muchdi then listened as the sound of the planes receded. But it is what he did not hear—gunfire from below—that comforted him most.

By the time the third C-130 approached the coast with Karsa Yudha 81 inside, they were 600 meters behind the lead plane. The two jumpmasters looked below, straining to ascertain any terrain feature. Seeing a strip of lighter gray and assuming it was beach-break, they let a pair of commandos enter into the slipstream on either side.

Lieutenant Subagyo, the *prayudha* commander, was third in his stick and ready to leap. At the last second, the jumpmaster stuck out his foot to block his exit. The light gray strip was either the wake of a boat or a large swell; the beach was still a few seconds of flight away.

Pausing long enough to be satisfied they were now over land, the

---

3   Suwito interview.

jumpmaster removed his foot and the rest of the stick exited the plane.[4]

*

Sergeant Ramedi, one of the commandos who jumped prematurely from the third aircraft, confirmed his chute was properly opened and then looked downward to get his bearings. To the north, he could see small, brief pinpricks of light: muzzle flashes from ground fire. Falintil had started to react.

But that was the least of his problems. To the north the ground was a dark gray; directly below him was a decidedly lighter shade of gray. He was over water.

Grabbing the toggles and doing his best to steer in a northerly direction, Ramedi prayed the natural forward momentum of his canopy during decent would be enough to carry him past the shoreline.

Thirty seconds later, Ramedi crashed into the surf. The parachute canopy came to rest behind him, dragging him backward and under the salty brine. Gaining his balance, he stood in knee-deep water. Still strapped in his parachute harness, he tapped into his energy reserves and clawed his way to dry land.

Donning his rucksack, Ramedi let his hands work their way over his AK-47 to ensure all felt in order. He then crossed the sand, silently disappearing into the jungle.

*

One of the last in his stick on the third plane, Lieutenant Alberto Nainggolan was dropped farthest inland and away from the beach. This was hardly a blessing, as flashes of gunfire could be seen directly below. Falintil was by now fully aware of the airborne drop, and they were taking shots at the parachutists silhouetted against the dawn sky.

Helpless under his main chute, Alberto flinched every time he heard the crack of a rifle round whistling upward. After a few seconds that seemed like an eternity, he landed amidst bamboo and rolled to a rest on the jungle floor. He immediately checked over his body to ensure there was no blood.[5]

Several other *sandi yudha* members had landed in the same bamboo thicket. They could hear the staccato rattle of gunfire in all directions. With their AK-47s at the ready, they began movement toward the runway.

---

4   Subagyo H.S. interview.
5   Interview with Alberto Nainggolan, 7 June 2016.

CHAPTER SIX - HELL IN A VERY, VERY SMALL PLACE

*

By the time the fourth C-130 filled with Karsa Yudha 82 approached the coast, Nanggala 8 was running short on luck. Making the same mistake as the third plane, its jumpmasters incorrectly interpreted the off-shore swells and let a pair of commandos prematurely exit the plane. This time, Warrant Officer Sunarpo and Corporal Sutisna (who had a premonition of his own fate the night before) never stood a chance. Landing 100 meters from shore, their heavy loads took them straight to the bottom. They were the first two fatalities of the operation.

As the rest of the sticks exited the C-130, they entered a maelstrom of Falintil gunfire. The hardest hit was Prayudha 3, which had drifted toward the southern edge of the runway. Two of its members, Sergeant Sukardjo and Sergeant Major Udin, were cut down in crossfire next to the airfield and bled to death.

A third member, Warrant Officer Wagimo, was still suspended in his harness from a mango tree when Falintil set upon him. Testimony differs as to whether he was beheaded or had his legs removed; all agree that his body was mutilated while dangling from the tree.[6]

*

Back at Penfui, the four C-130s landed at sunrise. Colonel Djasmin got out of his plane and saw Lt. Colonel Soegito, the Kopassandha group commander who had led Nanggala 5 into Dili two months earlier, waiting on the tarmac. Soegito had been lax in shaving over the previous few weeks, and now was looking like an Indonesian version of Errol Flynn in *Robin Hood*.

Soegito pointed at the fuselage of Djasmin's plane. They counted half a dozen bullet holes, a line of dark oil streaming out of one.[7]

Djasmin crossed to the terminal building in search of Colonel Sanif. Nanggala 8, he wanted to report, was meeting with a hostile reception.

*

With Nanggala 8 scattered across the forested drop-zone, its members attempted to sort out friend from foe as they made their way toward the

---

6   There have been persistent, and unfounded, rumors that one Kopassandha member was captured by Falintil near the airfield and taken into Suai town, only to be executed the next day.
7   Djasmin interview.

airstrip. The distance to the runway was short but harrowing, with shots ringing through the jungle from elusive armed Falintil and skittish Kopassandha colleagues. There was also a small river that weaved through the vicinity, but it was baked dry.

Lieutenant Muchdi waited an hour to gather nearly a platoon of his men before beginning movement north. Out of the brush, he heard his name being called. It was Captain Dolfi, the deputy head of Karsa Yudha 82. Dolfi had exited the C-130 gripping his AK-47, but the shock of the main chute deploying had sent it tumbling out of his hands.[8]

"Can I borrow your pistol?" asked Dolfi. Muchdi handed over his sidearm, not bothering to ask how that, too, had been lost.[9]

Closer to the runway, a large group from Karsa Yudha 81 had managed to coalesce. Among them, Lieutenant Alberto Nainggolan moved cautiously through the scrub and came across a prone Corporal Gintings writhing in pain from a bullet wound to the thigh. Gintings begged for some water, but Alberto was reluctant. He had recently watched a Western on television where the protagonist, suffering a gut wound, took a sip from a canteen and promptly expired. Though the situations were radically different, Alberto did not want to take any chances: he offered some words of encouragement to Gintings but refused to share his water.[10]

Edging closer to the runway, Alberto spied a Fretilin flag waving from the top of a bamboo pole. Not seeing any movement further north alongside the strip, he sprinted onto the runway, ripped down the Fretilin banner and replaced it with an Indonesian flag.

At 1000, Sergeant Suwito emerged from the bush at the southern edge of the airfield. By that time nearly 200 members of Nanggala 8 had reached the vicinity. Suwito also saw the bodies of his three deceased comrades, all wrapped in ponchos. Barely pausing, he joined one other sergeant and Lieutenant Umpusinga as they worked their way through the jungle up the eastern side of the runway.

After progressing for half a kilometer, the three heard a noise and froze. Through the foliage, they could see a pair of huts. A man on a horse, seemingly oblivious to what had transpired over the previous several hours, was approaching one of the dwellings. The Kopassanda team fired off a volley

---

8 Captain Dolfi was not the only member to lose his assault rifle in midair: at least eleven were lost during the jump. This was likely the result of commandos attempting to parachute while holding their firearms so as to engage Falintil while dropping. Subagyo, p. 74.
9 Dolfi interview; Muchdi interview.
10 Alberto Nainggolan interview.

from their AK47s, killing the rider. A single Timorese male then emerged from the hut and sprinted for the tree-line, but was also cut down.

Approaching the hut, the commandos kicked in the door and peered inside. An elderly Timorese man stared at them, resigned to his fate. The commandos left him alone, but retrieved two rifles—one Getme, one Mauser—and headed back south.[11]

By noon, save for a handful of stragglers still lost in the bush, nearly all of Nanggala 8 had assembled at the runway. The two *karsa yudha* gathered on the western side; the para-commando company massed on the east. The runway itself had been blocked with bamboo spikes (to impale parachutists) and drums of sand.

Major Soekiman took stock of the situation. The lead elements from Task Force Sikatan, contacted over the radio, still had another 15 kilometers to go; the UDT partisans were nowhere to be found.

Placing a call to Kupang, Soekiman told Colonel Sanif they would start removing obstacles from the runway so resupply flights could land later that afternoon. Eager to assess the situation himself, Sanif said he was on the way in a Pelita chopper.

By the time Sanif arrived, the runway had been largely cleared. Word was passed back to Kupang, which readied a C-47 resupply flight with tins of fried rice and ammunition. There were also upwards of a dozen wounded commandos who needed evacuation.

While Sanif was pleased that the runway was under control—and thus no long available to the UN envoys—the disposition of Falintil left him uncomfortable. Whatever armed opposition had been located around the drop-zone had disappeared without a trace, presumably retreating west into Suai town. As Failintil had access to larger caliber weaponry than Nanggala 8, this left the commandos exceedingly vulnerable around the runway.

Turning to Soekiman, Sanif ordered Nanggala 8 to move west into Suai. Their eastern flank, meantime, would be swept by Task Force Sikatan as they slowly progressed toward a rendezvous.

As directed, Soekiman assigned his deputy, Captain Warow, with defending the runway using half of the each *karsa yudha*. Soekiman himself would take the rest of Nanggala 8 toward Suai, with the para-commando company in the lead.

Marching along a narrow dirt road southwest from the airstrip, the scene was eerily desolate. Not a villager was in sight as the commandos cautiously

---

11 Suwito interview.

covered one kilometer to a road junction. To the west, Suai was another 2 kilometers. What few huts they encountered along this stretch, too, were abandoned.

Rounding a bend in the road, they arrived at the village of Debos on the southeastern outskirts of Suai. Here the huts gave way to a handful of white-washed concrete buildings, along with the telltale spire of the obligatory church. The lead para-commandos leap-frogged past each other, halting near the side of the church. Peering around the corner, for the first time they spotted inhabitants: armed males, taking up positions around a hut cluster a few hundred meters to their west.

Instinctively, the commandos unleashed a volley of AK-47 rounds. Falintil responded in kind with assault rifles and a machine gun, the bullets absorbed by the church's concrete edifice.

No sooner had Soekiman moved up to the church when a mortar round landed nearby and sent shards of mortar and stone across the commando line. Soekiman looked back in disgust: the mortar had come from their own tubes farther east. Turning to a radioman, he growled an order for them to adjust fire.[12]

A few minutes later, the Falintil gunfire stopped. Continuing forward, slower this time, the commandos pressed through Debos. Passing an abandoned shop, several of them went inside and found stocks of soybean milk and corn. Having not eaten in a day, the famished soldiers quickly feasted.

Past the western edge of Debos, the commando column spied a large villa atop a slight rise. Thirteen men, including Soekiman, Captain Moeryono, and Lieutenant Muchdi, slowly approached the stone wall surrounding the residence. They had barely taken cover when Falintil unleashed a new round of bullets.

The number of Falintil was probably not large, likely no more than a platoon. But in the ensuing standoff, Nanggala 8 was hopelessly outgunned. Their AK-47s had a range out to 350 meters, but Falintil's Getme was effective to 500 meters. Falintil had also started a lop-sided mortar duel, significantly outsizing the tiny 50mm rounds used by Kopassandha.

Trying to get a fix on the Falintil firing positions, Corporal Sudiman—Muchdi's adjutant who had been released from the brig—peered over the top of the wall. A Getme round instantly went through his forehead, blowing open his skull. Sudiman collapsed to Muchdi's right.

Pinned down for another hour, Warrant Officer Suyitno, the commander

---

12   Suwito interview.

of 1st Platoon, defiantly stood up. Falintil answered by placing a round through his gut. Suyitno dropped in a heap to Muchdi's left, his lifeblood pulsing out from his stomach. Three other Kopassandha were also shot and wounded.

Two hours later, with ammunition running low, the commandos decided to make one last attempt to rush through the villa and seize the high ground. But just as they began to mount the wall, they saw a pair of Timorese in the distance, expertly firing rifles while galloping on horses. "It was like a scene from *Taras Bulba*," said Suwito, referencing a 1962 film about Cossack horsemen.[13]

Fearing a mounted attack, the Nanggala 8 column retraced its steps east through Debos with the two fatalities, then continued back to the airfield at last light. Ammunition and tins filled with fried rice—Indonesia's answer to the C-Ration—had been air-dropped and air-landed during the preceding hours, allowing them to ward off their hunger pangs. The lead element of Sikatan had also arrived at the runway, with the remainder of the column expected by no later than the following afternoon. Using rucksacks for pillows, the commandos sprawled out along the edges of the airstrip and got their first good sleep in forty-eight hours.

*

As dawn broke on 5 February, the food and rest filled the members of Nanggala 8 with fresh resolve. Too, virtually the entire Sikatan column had reached the runway, finally giving them mortars on par with Falintil.

With the bulk of Nanggala 8 in the lead, at noon they once more headed down the road toward Debos. A second column, consisting of an infantry company from Sikatan and a *sandi yudha* team, went further south to seize the small port at Suailoro village.[14]

This time, Falintil had pragmatically decided to fight another day on their own terms. As the commandos pressed through Debos and into the center of Suai, they found a ghost town. Except for one Timorese corpse, not a single inhabitant could be found.

Even the ethnic Chinese shopkeepers, a robust lot who weathered most conflicts in place, had elected to take to the bush. A *sandi yudha* team entered one of their abandoned gold shops, a case of chains still on display.[15]

The same results were found at the Suailoro pier, which had already been

---

13 *Ibid.*
14 *Laporan Operasi Seroja*, p. 25.
15 Subagyo H.S. interview.

abandoned by Falintil defenders. Exploring, the *sandi yudha* troops came across several primitive oil wells near the beach, the sticky pitch used for lamp fuel.

Setting up a command post in Debos, Soekiman got on the radio to Sanif in Kupang. All of their objectives had been seized, he reported, and Failintil had presumably retreated west toward Tilomar or Fohorem sub-districts.

In the background, a squad of para-commandos, letting down their guard for the first time in two days, were busy wrangled some goats found wandering through the dusty streets of Debos. Tonight, they would not be settling for more tins of fried rice.

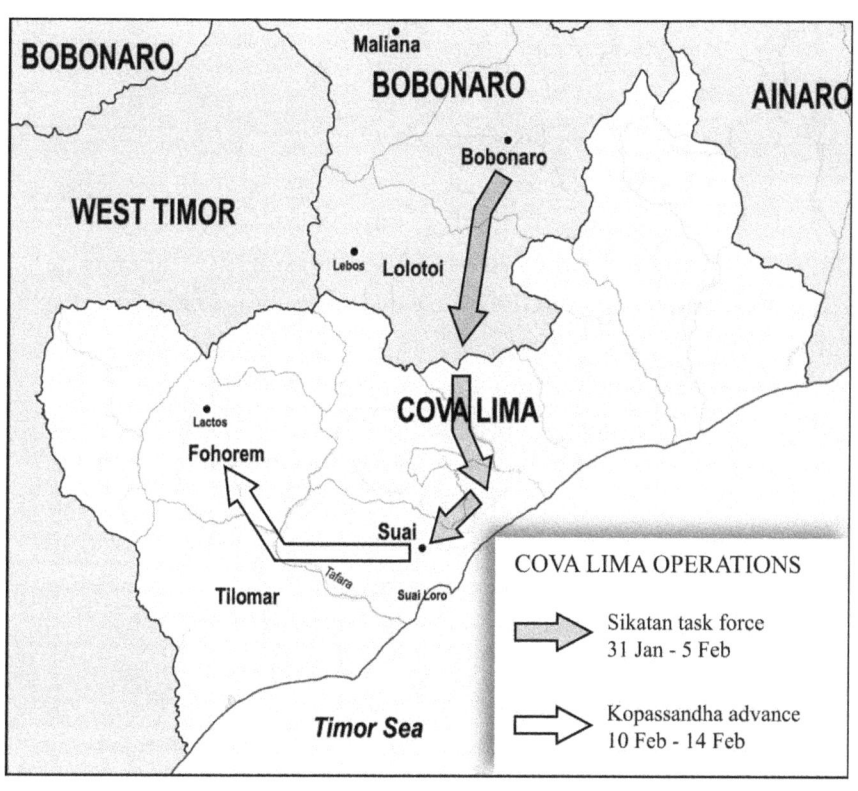

CHAPTER SEVEN
LACTOS INTOLERANT

The timing of the Indonesian press releases was impeccable. On the morning of 4 February, Jakarta's PGET proxy magnanimously announced that they would allow the UN delegation to land on Timor's southern coast. The catch: the Portuguese corvette transporting them had to hoist the UN flag and not get closer than four nautical miles. Moreover, only four persons could go ashore in a skiff, and they had to give advance notice of the time and place.[1]

Just a few hours later, the reason for the PGET's change of heart became apparent when they issued a second press statement detailing fifteen locations that had recently been liberated. The first on the list: Suai. For good measure, the PGET repeated their threat to shoot down any unauthorized aircraft entering Timorese airspace.[2]

Hearing of the PGET's acquiescence toward the use of the Portuguese corvette, Winspeare declared that the terms were acceptable in theory. In practice, however, Fretilin had yet to come up with a suitable rendezvous location.

Things only got more confusing on 5 February, when Australia belatedly gave permission for Fretilin representatives to use Telecom facilities in addition to the radio on the *João Roby*. After a series of short exchanges over both sets during the ensuing day, Ramos-Horta concluded that a sea landing was too dangerous. He then returned to the tired refrain that the UN representatives could fly to Suai, Same, Viqueque, or Com—this despite the fact that Australia

---

1   FBIS, Asia and Pacific edition, 5 February 1976, p. M2.
2   FBIS, Asia and Pacific edition, 6 February 1976, p. Q1.

was still banning all flights to Timor and there was mounting evidence all those location were, in fact, already under Indonesian control.[3]

Winspeare was not buying this dated narrative, and apparently neither was Ramos-Horta. The latter departed Darwin late on 6 February for Melbourne, with the stated intent to head for Lisbon. The exit of Ramos-Horta brought a de facto end to further consideration of meeting with Fretilin inside Timor. The Australians, for one, were relieved over this. Their Minister for Foreign Affairs, Andrew Peacock, shed a crocodile tear or two while lauding Winspeare for having done "everything that could be reasonably expected of him to establish contact with Fretilin leaders."[4]

Such praise offered little consolation to the prickly Italian. On 7 February, a livid Winspeare flew from Darwin to Sydney to brief UN Secretary General Waldheim, who coincidentally was scheduled to land the following morning for a three-day visit to Australia. En route, Winspeare spoke candidly with his Australian diplomatic escort, unleashing venom in all directions. Fretilin was wasting his time, he complained, and the Portuguese were to blame for having dragged their heels on a de-colonization schedule.

His sharpest barbs, however, were reserved for the Indonesians. Foreign Minister Malik was "an accomplished liar," he said, and Suharto was a "little general" with the mentality of an accountant. By contrast, Winspeare felt General Ali Moertopo, an intelligence officer whose expertise was social engineering (and whose Operation Komodo had failed miserably in Portuguese Timor), was "the power" in Indonesia. He claimed that Moertopo's people had tried repeatedly to bribe or compromise their delegation in crude fashion, such as by throwing a lavish dinner party during their 22 January transit in Bali and pressuring them to except expensive gifts of paintings.[5]

Winspeare relayed these sentiments on 8 February when he huddled with Waldheim. The next day, a Fretilin representative attempted to pass Winspeare a message that a visit to Timor could still possibly be arranged. As usual, the offer was short on specifics. By then it mattered little, as the UN delegation was already winging its way back to Geneva.[6]

---

3   *The Canberra Times*, 7 February 1976, p. 1, 7; Way, p. 700.
4   U.S. Department of State message #0540, UN Mission (New York) to Secretary of State, 12 February 1976.
5   Way, p. 704. Winspeare's frustration may have led him to somewhat embellish the Indonesian attempts to win his favor. Jensen recalls being presented with a painting after the 22 January dinner, but believes it was no more than standard tourist ware of no great value. He also recalls having to insist that they pay their Bali hotel bill, but without causing any great fanfare. Jensen correspondence.
6   Way, p. 700.

After the short, intense fighting of 4 February, Nanggala 8 spent the next five days enjoying relative inactivity while hunkered down in Suai. The *sandi yudha* officers had taken up residence in abandoned homes, while the more austere para-commandos pitched clusters of tents. All of them used the time to relay messages back to loved ones on Java that they were in good health. One especially poignant transmission was sent by Lieutenant Alberto Nainggolan to his heavily pregnant wife. Referencing his recent combat, he urged her to pick the name Debos if she gave birth to a son, and Suaiti in the event they had a daughter.[7]

Only a handful of Timorese civilians had filtered back from the bush in the interim, and all were giving the Kopassandha troopers a wide berth. Falintil was also giving them a wide berth, with one exception. A team of innovative guerrillas had fixed a large mortar to the back of a Unimog truck. Near dusk, they would race up to the town's western edge and lob some rounds before disappearing back into the bush. The commandos manning the town's perimeter could hear its engine rumbling along the nearby jungle trails at night, but were reluctant to give chase on Falintil's home turf.[8]

On the morning of 10 February, Soekiman gathered his officers to announce their siesta was over. Kogasgab had handed down orders to sweep the western half of Cova Lima district, he announced, and Nanggala 8 was to immediately head west along with Infantry Battalion 507 (which had been the core of Task Force Sikatan). They were to set off for the Tafara River, where the infantry would cross and take Tilomar sub-district. Kopassandha would veer northwest, ford the Tafara near its headwaters, and move toward Lactos village in the center of Forohem sub-district.

Though only 20 kilometers from Suai, the trek to Lactos promised to be a grueling slog through winding jungle trails highly susceptible to guerrilla ambush. This was the same kind of conventional operation that had drained their Nanggala 5 colleagues during the march from Dili to Aileu in late 1975. At best, it was a waste of highly trained commandos in a role that could just as easily be performed by regular infantry. At worst, the lightly-armed Kopassandha column would again be out-gunned by their Falintil opponents.

Their initial movement during the second half of 10 February was easy enough. Falintil was cooperative, initiating some light contact but generally

---

7   Alberto Nainggolan interview.
8   Suwito interview.

staying ahead of the Indonesians and retreating across the Tafara. They were forced to abandon their Unimog on the eastern side of the river, which the approaching para-commandos finished off with a rocket round.[9]

At that point the infantry battalion divided into two columns and continued west, fording the Tafara and pushing deep into Tilomar. Along the way they ran into a few Falintil pockets, killing a dozen and captured forty-two suspected guerrillas.[10]

Nanggala 8, meantime, pivoted to the northwest. Early on 11 February, the razor-sharp savanna grass mercifully gave way to lush, rolling fields. Very soon they came across dozens of cows in what was once a cattle ranch abandoned by the former Cova Lima district chief. The free-ranging bovines appeared to be faring nicely, and the commandos paused long enough to partake in a steak barbeque.

Staying on a course roughly parallel to the Tafara on their left, by midday Nanggala 8 had reached a juncture in the river. The Tafara was little more than a slightly swollen stream at that point, presenting only a minor obstacle. But mindful of a possible Falintil ambush on the opposite bank, the commandos took up cover and sent over a handful of scouts. The rest of the column awaited their turn to rush across in small numbers, dragging out the crossing to a couple of hours.

Entering Forohem sub-district, the terrain changed dramatically. Timor's interior was far more mountainous and steamy than the parched coast, rightly earning the moniker "Tropical Switzerland." There were no proper roads through that section of Forohem, but the vicinity was crisscrossed by narrow cart paths. It did not take long for Nanggala 8 to come across a trail on their desired northwestern heading. Channeled along a trail in that manner, of course, made the column exceedingly vulnerable to ambush. This was not lost on Soekiman, who concentrated the para-commandos and their heavier weapons near the front of the column.

Nanggala 8 also had to contend with food issues. Each member had been provided with several tins of fried rice which, monotony aside, provided a dose of carbohydrates with only limited nutritional value. And as there were no contingencies to airdrop rations into the jungle while they were on the march, the commandos resorted to foraging along the way for papaya, grapefruit,

---

9 Suwito interview.
10 *Tiga Puluh Tahun Bhakti Divisi Infanteri 2/Kostrad, 1961-1991, Tim Penyusun Sejarah Divisi Infanteri 2/Kostrad, 1991*, p. 253. During this period, Infantry Brigade 2 captured Fretilin's deputy head for the Suai vicinity, Domingus Baros, and the Fretilin secretary for Suai, Moses de Jesus. *Laporan Operasi Seroja*, p. 20.

and cassava root. They also chanced upon a feral horse, adding some protein to their diet.[11]

With nightfall approaching, Nanggala 8 edged off of the trail and looked for cover. They had been fortunate, marching for an entire day without any contact by fire. The men were physically drained and, aside from those rotating on sentry duty, they attempted to get some rest despite the chill, hunger, leeches, and mosquitos. None of this especially fazed Lieutenant Muchdi, who curled up inside a depression in the hillside and began to snore loudly.

As 12 February dawned, Nanggala 8 re-assembled along the trail to continue their trek toward the northwest. Almost immediately, they triggered the first Falintil ambush. Getme rounds cut through the foliage, filling the air with leaf confetti. The 2nd Platoon of para-commandos was at the head of the column and took the brunt of the attack. They instinctively moved off the path and attempted to find cover, but few of the trees had enough girth to afford adequate concealment. Worse, the thick vegetation and overhead canopy precluded a response from their mortars or rockets.

Pinned down in place, an RPD gunner opened up and chewed holes into the jungle. This silenced Falintil for a moment, only to have them resume from a different direction. Muchdi worked his way up the column, imploring his para-commandos to continue forward movement in order to work their way out of the ambush zone. This had only limited effect, as their progress was measured in mere meters through the afternoon.

Not until dusk did the Falintil fire peter out, allowing Nanggala 8 could properly attend to half a dozen of their wounded. Performing a headcount, they discovered two missing: Warrant Officer Tukiman, the commander of 2nd Platoon, and his assistant, Corporal Abdul Wahid. Both had been at the front of the column when they hit the ambush, and neither had been seen since. Their bodies were presumably in the nearby jungle, but recovery patrols could not be sent out in the fading light.[12]

Saddened by their losses, the commandos prepared a perimeter defense so they could get some much-needed rest. As they were doing so, a final volley of Getme rounds punctuated the night. One of the sentries, Corporal Ashuri, collapsed with a fatal round to the head. His colleagues pulled back, cursing their unseen Timorese opponents. They wanted to retrieve Ashuri's body but, knowing Falintil was lurking nearby and would probably inflict further casualties on the recovery party, Soekiman ordered them to stand down. It was

---

11 Suwito interview; Muchdi interview.
12 Neither body was ever found. Suwito interview.

a gut-wrenching ending to a monumentally bad day.

*

As the sun rose on 13 February, Falintil offered no reprieve. No sooner had Nanggala 8 resumed movement northwest, they hit their first ambush. This was even more determined than the previous day, scattering the commandos for a time in the jungle.

Corporal Triyanto, separated from his squad in the confusion, lost his footing and rolled down a small embankment. As he searched for his AK-47 in the leaf litter, a Falintil guerrilla materialized from the foliage. The Timorese was holding a native ax above his head, prompting Triyanto to turn tail and attempt to sprint back up the embankment. The guerrilla was faster, however, closing the gap to the commando and bringing down the ax on Triyanto's shoulder. The corporal was saved by his rucksack, which only allowed a fraction of the blade to slice into his flesh.

With the ax handle hanging off his back, Triyanto wrestled free and rocketed into the bush. But in the confrontation he had lost his bearings. Not stopping until the sound of gunfire was in the far distance, he paused to remove his blood-soaked rucksack.

Hopelessly lost, Triyanto's struggles were just beginning. As his back injury festered and his energy waned, he spent days, then weeks, walking in what he thought was a southeastern direction. Relying on his survival skills, he foraged for insects and edible vegetation, moving cautiously so as not to run into a Falintil patrol. Not until a full two months later did a heavily emaciated Triyanto manage to safely reach an infantry outpost on the outskirts of Suai.

*

For the rest of Nanggala 8, they managed to regroup and take stock of their losses late on the afternoon of 13 February. Triyanto was missing and presumed dead, while a dozen had suffered a range of battle-related injuries. They still had another three kilometers to go before reaching Lactos, and the fighting had devolved into an ugly slugfest in which their AK-47s were being routinely bested by the longer-range Getme.

After getting a few short hours of sleep, Soekiman passed word during the pre-dawn hours of 14 February that he wanted the column ready to move by 0530. Mobilizing in the dark, they covered the first kilometer without incident.

Still two kilometers short of Lactos, the terrain opened up as the head of the column mounted a hilltop in the morning mist. Half a kilometer in front of them on an adjacent hill they could see a trio of stone pig pens, each about four by four meters in size and spaced twenty meters apart. The walls of the pens were around 1.5 meters in height and topped by a thatched roof. Given their solid construction, and the fact that they dominated the high ground, they looked suspiciously like pillboxes.

Soekiman squinted at the structures in the distance and had misgivings. But as the pens were situated between them and Lactos, he decided there was no other option than to rush them sequentially in order to clear out of any concealed Falintil.

In single file, a squad of commandos sprinted ahead and reached the wall of the first pen. Maneuvering to approach the pen's entrance, Sergeant Suwito did not take notice of the ventilation gaps in the stone edifice. When Suwito attempted to peer inside, a Falintil guerrilla inside poked his Getme barrel through one of the gaps. As it came in contact with Suwito's leg, a shot rang out and blew off a sizable portion of the commando's left thigh.

As Suwito collapsed in pain, the rest of his squad rushed forward and sprayed gunfire. Four Falintil corpses were later removed. Suwito himself was evacuated that afternoon by helicopter to a field hospital across the border inside Indonesia; 96 stiches and 28 days later, he was put on a plane to fully recuperate in Jakarta. Due to ongoing sensitivities about Kopassandha's involvement in Timor and losses they had incurred, he was forbidden from contacting kin during his convalescence.[13]

For the other two pig pens, rocket launchers were brought forward to put them out of commission at a safer distance. Each was found to be empty. This allowed Nanggala 8 to then walk the remaining short distance into the empty, seemingly inconsequential village of Lactos. While they had claimed their prize, it was at heavy cost in terms of dead and wounded. Kopassandha, yet again, had been improperly wielded as light infantry.

Meantime, Falintil in true guerrilla fashion faded into the jungle and did not further challenge Nanggala 8's hold over Lactos. An infantry unit backed by heavy weapons arrived two days later, allowing the bloodied and battered commandos to retrace their steps toward the relative comforts of Suai.

*

---

13 *Ibid.*

While Nanggala 8 had been battling its way across Cova Lima, a separate battle was taking place on the airwaves in and out of Timor. On the Fretilin side, Australia on 11 February had withdrawn permission for Tony Belo to continue using the Telecom transmitter. Taking its place, a network of pro-Fretilin sympathizers began shuttling unlicensed radio sets around the outback near Darwin to stay a step ahead of the authorities.

On 14 February, one of these sets received a message purporting to be from the Fretilin leadership hunkered down in Timor's mountainous interior. Long on hyperbole, the message admitted 300 paratroopers had been dropped on Suai, but claimed most were eliminated by Falintil. The message further claimed they were putting up strong resistance in the Suai vicinity.[14]

A day earlier, Jakarta's PGET proxy had issued its own statement with an invitation for Winspeare and his delegation to visit Suai, Same, Viqueque, and Com—the exact locations Fretilin had earlier proposed as meeting sites. All of these venues, the PGET noted, were now under its "territorial jurisdiction."[15]

For his part, Winspeare and his team returned to Geneva and got to work sorting out their findings. Much of the writing was left to Jensen, who had a polished draft to Winspeare by the last week of the month. On 29 February, this was handed over to Secretary General Waldheim.

Not surprisingly, Ramos-Horta, who had skulked off to Lisbon, was less than complimentary about the envoy's conclusions. "Bland, cautious, ambiguous," were the adjectives he used to describe them.[16]

Equally unsurprising, Jensen defended the report and later recalled how realpolitik of the day had shaped opinion against Fretilin:

> ...it is easy now to forget that in 1976 both the U.S. and the Soviets saw Indonesia as important and had no wish to antagonize it. Britain looked to back Australia, which was very quick to recognize Indonesia's action in Timor. France remained on the sidelines. China supported Fretilin warmly in the Council but from confidential conversations I concluded, and Winspeare agreed, that China would not intervene directly or supply arms.[17]

None were happier about this than Jakarta, which had dodged a proverbial bullet by avoiding any major gaffs during Winspeare's meetings with the PGET and successfully frustrating any attempts by him to meet Fretilin's leadership in the jungles of Timor.

---

14 *Timor Information Service*, No. 8, 12 March 1976.
15 "Report by the Secretary-General in Pursuance of Security Council Resolution 384," p. 1.
16 Ramos-Horta, p. 118.
17 Jensen correspondence.

With regard to the latter, Nanggala 8's role had been instrumental—and Kopassandha commander Yogie Memet years later lauded their effort. "Suai was the largest airborne operation by Kopassandha," he would recount to one military historian. "And it was their mission of which I was most proud." [18]

---

[18] Atmadji interview.

CHAPTER EIGHT
THUNDERCLAP

Arriving back at Suai, Nanggala 8 set up perimeter around town and awaited an infantry battalion to replace them. Arriving at long last, too, was the UDT platoon led by Rui Lopes. Though he was too late to assist with the fighting around Suai, Rui had earned favor among the Indonesian top brass for his diehard loyalty; as a reward, he would later be named the Cova Lima district chief.

The down time for Nanggala 8 in Suai was cathartic, as morale was low among the commandos. This was especially true among the two *karsa yudha*, whose men were bristling at being misused during the march to Lactos and back. Their original raison d'être, after all, was to act as guerrillas in the event Indonesia was overrun by a conventional communist juggernaut; instead, they themselves had become the conventional juggernaut—and were on the receiving end of a deadly insurgent response. Worse, Failintil was showing excellent fire discipline and accuracy, the result of compulsory military service enforced by the Portuguese.

In the end, the wait in Suai extended to more than a month. Among many in Nanggala 8, this provided their first real exposure to ethnic Timorese. For Lieutenant Alberto Nainggolan—whose wife gave birth to their son, Debos, on 5 March—his first impression was exceedingly positive:

> I met a 20-year old Timorese in Suai named Agus. He was six years younger than me, and seemed very friendly and loyal. We did confidence-building measures to test him, and finally gave him a rifle—with just one bullet—and sent him on patrols around the perimeter.[1]

---

1   Alberto Nainggolan interview.

Agus proved to be the exception rather than the rule, however. For the most part, the Timorese, during the rare instances they interacted with the Indonesian military, were relegated to menial coolie labor. Even the Apodeti and UDT militia, trained and armed prior to Seroja, were quickly being relegated to coolie status.

Near the end of March, Kogasgab finally got around to sending an East Java infantry battalion to take over security in Suai. As the original plan called for Nanggala 8 to serve a seven-month tour in East Timor, this meant they needed another assignment for the next five months. Given Nanggala 8's large size, Kogasgab decided to split them apart: Karsa Yudha 82 would go to Baucau and conduct intelligence-gathering in the eastern sector, Karsa Yudha 81 would go to Dili and do the same in the central sector, and the para-commando company would go to Dili to act as Kogasgab's mobile reserve.

As Nanggala 8 packed in preparation to leave Suai on 1 April, Jakarta sent them a parting message. On account of their successful seizure of the Suai runway, nearly all of its members received an extraordinary promotion in rank. On that positive note, the unit took skiffs out to a lumbering transport ship from the state-owned shipping line Pelni. Steaming around the eastern tip of Timor and anchoring off Baucau, Karsa Yudha 82 went ashore.[2]

Almost as soon as they arrived, Sudiyono, the Karsa Yudha 82 commander, was ordered to report to Java to attend a training course; his position was taken over by his deputy, Dolfi Rondonuwu. Of the four *prayudya*, two remained in Baucau, one was sent to Ossu sub-district to the south, and one went to Los Palos (which had been seized by the airborne infantry on 3 February) to the east.[3]

In these new environs, all four *prayudha* finally began to engage in special warfare missions. Much of this centered on re-building a civil infrastructure. Recalled one of the *prayudha* commanders in Baucau, Captain Umpusinga:

> We had to convince the populace to come out of hiding in the mountains, for example by using loudspeakers, and then we had to help escort them back to Baucau. We then had to help them select a district chief from among themselves. We didn't leave until the Baucau district administration was up and running.[4]

Meantime, the Nanggala 8 command staff, Karsa Yudha 81, and the para-commando company had continued west aboard the Pelni ship. Upon reaching

---

2   Nanggala 4 under Major Sofyan Effendi, which had been fighting in Timor since Operation Flamboyan, got aboard in Baucau for the trip back to Java. Muchdi interview.
3   Dolfi interview. Shortly after returning to Jakarta, Major Sudiyono collapsed and died of kidney failure during a morning run in Cijantung.
4   Interview with Hakim Saleh Umpusinga, 8 April 2017.

Dili, they docked and all went ashore.⁵

Dili had changed little in the two months since the Winspeare visit, with much of the town still left vacant by the departing Portuguese administrators and entrepreneurial class. The Nanggala 8 command staff took up residence in an abandoned house in Colmera, a neighborhood near the town's port. The para-commandos, meantime, initially set up camp at the *Quartel General*, the old *Tropas* headquarters on the southern outskirts of town. Two days later they shifted to Hera sub-district, immediately east of Dili. From there, Captain Muchdi began sending patrols along the eastern approaches into Dili. Falintil ambushes remained a constant threat, even that close to town. On 5 April, less than a week after arriving, one of the patrols got into an intense firefight; Sergeant Maman took a round and bled to death before getting to a hospital.⁶

For Karsa Yudha 81, its headquarters staff took over a house near the *Quartel General*, while its *prayudha* were spread across town. Captain Subaygo, one of the newly-promoted *prayudha* commanders, managed to appropriate an abandoned white Datsun sedan, which reportedly belonged to Fretilin President Nicholau Lobato.⁷ Not to be outdone, Alberto Nainggolan—also now sporting the rank of captain—liberated another Datsun sedan and adopted the nickname "The Lobato Kid." ⁸

As was the case with Karsa Yudha 82 to the east, the *prayudha* in Dili started to get unconventional assignments more in line with their expertise. This included setting up informant networks and conducting undercover raids for illegal weapons. This was no easy feat, especially given the language and cultural barrier that left a sizable rift between the Timorese and Indonesian troops.

Before they had a chance to show much progress, Soekiman handed down orders on 22 April for an ambitious operation to sweep Dili of all Fretilin cells. Specifically, there were indications Fretilin agents planned to force residents of the Becora neighborhood in Dili's southeastern corner to evacuate to the

---

5   Nanggala 3 under Major Tarub, which had been fighting in Timor since Operation Flamboyan, boarded in Dili. Together with Nanggala 4 that had boarded in Baucau, they both headed back to Java on the Pelni vessel. Muchdi interview.
6   Muchdi's para-commando company replaced elements of Nanggala 5 at Hera led by Captain Luhut Pandjaitan; the latter were then able to return to Cijantung. *Ibid.*
7   According to a Fretilin source, the white Datsun actually belonged to Jose Goncalves, who had been named the Fretilin Minister for Economy and Statistics in November 1975. Interview with Alberto X.P. Carlos, 30 May 2017.
8   Lobato had been named prime minister when Fretilin declared independence on 28 November 1975. Just over a week later when Seroja kicked off on 7 December, he changed his title from prime minister to president.

countryside. Karsa Yudha 81 was to frustrate these plans in an operation codenamed *Guntur* (Indonesian for "Thunderclap").[9]

Like the name suggested, Guntur kicked off with sufficient shock value. Dressed in civilian attire, the *sandi yudha* troops blitzed across town and began arresting suspected Fretilin sympathizers. Two Fretilin agents were killed, one in possession of a Mauser. The biggest fish they managed to catch was Jose de Araujo, the head of Fretilin's Suai sector who had slipped out of that town when Nanggala 8 did their airborne assault during February.

Not all of the *sandi yudha* operations were within Dili. During June, Soekiman got orders to fully pacify the Oecussi enclave. Centuries earlier, Oecussi had been a key Portuguese foothold in Timor. But after the Dutch and Portuguese agreed to roughly divide the island in half, Oecussi became an 814-square kilometer divot of Portuguese territory isolated in the Dutch western zone. Why Lisbon bothered retaining control was not readily apparent: Timor was their colonial backwater, and Oecussi soon became their backwater's backwater. When Winspeare had visited in January, he reeled at the primitive conditions that seemed to have changed little over hundreds of years.

Though under-developed, Portugal had seen to Oecussi's defenses. One of the four *Tropas* hunter companies was permanently stationed in the enclave as of mid-1975. In addition, a *Secunda Luna* militia company was kept there on a three-month rotating basis.[10]

These defenses had not fazed Indonesia during the run-up to Seroja. Starting in June 1975, pro-Indonesia militia began making regular forays into Oecussi. On 29 November, one day after Fretilin declared independence and a week before the airborne assault on Dili, UDT partisans were sufficiently ensconced in the enclave to raise an Indonesian flag over its capital town, Vila Taveiro.

But ever since then, Oecussi had been largely overlooked as Seroja unfolded. Jakarta could no longer afford such neglect, however, after indications that Jose Valente, a local leader and former head of *Tropas* troops in the enclave, was looking to forge a neutral path separate from the PGET. Valente had access to a sizable armory, up to and including mortars and bazookas, to back up his plan.

To neutralize Valente and take possession of the Oecussi armory, Soekiman tapped two *prayudha*. The catch: he wanted no casualties and, if at all possible, to avoid any shots being fired. This obviously called for use

---

9   Subagyo, pp. 77-78.
10 Grao correspondence.

of deception rather than brute force. To achieve this, the *sandi yudha* troops borrowed uniforms from the police and Indonesian territorial militia so as not to put Valente on edge. One of the *prayudha* then departed ahead of time by land, the other half synchronizing their arrival aboard a light plane. When the latter landed, a group of former *Tropas* approached the runway to investigate. As predicted, the *sandi yudha* disguised as militia seemed sufficiently non-threatening.

Continuing with the ruse, the commandos asked to pay a courtesy call on Valente. Taken to a villa near the beach, they tried to appear relaxed as the *Tropas* officer appeared. The eldest member of Karsa Yudha 81—who came across as a wizened, middle-aged bureaucrat—had been designated as their leader, and he began to chat up Valente and put the latter at ease. At that point, Captain Subagyo pulled a pistol and in a hushed tone ordered Valente to surrender.[11]

With Valente contained, the rest of the garrison put up no resistance. This was fortuitous, as the two *prayudha* seized a treasure trove of weapons—including hundreds of rifles, two mortars, and four 3.5-inch bazookas—which could have fueled a prolonged resistance had Valente continued in that direction.

*

While Operation Guntur and the Oecussi foray were efforts to use the *prayudha* in something closer to a true *sandi yudha* mission, Captain Hendropriyono remained less than impressed. The captain had been finishing a training course in Bandung when his Karsa Yudha 81 parachuted into Suai and battled its way to Lactos. He arrived on the scene just as his men, still seeing red from their perceived misuse, were streaming back into Suai.

Though he had missed out on that fight, Hendropriyono was no stranger to combat. His baptism by fire, in fact, had taken place during early 1968 in the jungles of West Kalimantan. Those were still early days in the counter-insurgency campaign against ethnic Chinese guerrillas that previously had done Jakarta's bidding. As a young lieutenant fresh from commando training, he spent the ensuing year—as his commander had instructed all new officers—"learning how to fight."

In late 1972, Captain Hendropriyono headed back to West Kalimantan for a second tour. This time, he was assigned as intelligence officer for Task

---
11 Subagyo H.S. interview.

Force 42. Doing double-duty, he was also put in charge of a special eight-man intelligence team—codenamed *Halilintar*, Indonesian for "Lightning"—that was to be the tip of the task force's counter-insurgency spear.

Though somewhat weakened by more than five consecutive years of battle against a better-armed Indonesian military, the ethnic Chinese insurgents in West Kalimantan remained formidable. This was true for several reasons. First, there was the overriding ethnic component to the conflict. A few centuries earlier, Chinese had come to Kalimantan by the thousands to work the island's gold mines. Their descendants formed large and highly cohesive Chinese communities across West Kalimantan, including about a third of the population around Pontianak and more than half of those living near Singkawang. This community offered sanctuary to the communist guerrillas, either out of ethnic solidarity or intimidation.

Second, the guerrillas had already spent about a decade operating as underground cells in Malaysia and had perfected tradecraft for clandestine communications. This included widespread use of dead-drops, with messages usually written in coded Chinese. Their disciplined cell structure and uses of aliases, too, complicated efforts to unravel their network.

Third, the West Kalimantan geography was dominated by thick jungle and swamps. Moreover, it was close to the Malaysian border, and the guerrillas often took advantage of jurisdictions by fleeing across the national boundary.

As the task force intelligence officer, Hendropriyono had to conjure news ways of overcoming these challenges. One of his biggest epiphanies ran counter to the prevailing mentality of racking up a high body count: he wanted guerrillas captured alive so he could extract information and, with luck and persistence, convert them into cooperative allies. Corpses, he argued, would not accomplish either of these goals.[12]

As more guerrillas were taken prisoner, Hendorpriyono began to painstakingly piece together an organizational chart of the underground movement across West Kalimantan. He would then send out his Halilintar team to make another snatch, and from that add more names to the chart.

One especially elusive figure was a wily ideologue named Siauw Ah San, the head of the communist sector encompassing Pontianak municipality.

---

12 Another part of what became a successful counter-insurgency strategy in West Kalimantan was to incite communal violence between the Chinese and ethnic Dayak tribesmen that constituted a sizable part of the same province. In an intelligence operation codenamed *Mangkok Merah* ("Red Bowl"), the murder of some ethnic Dayak villagers was pinned on the Chinese, sparking a ferocious pogrom by the Dayak that sent many rural Chinese fleeing to government-held enclaves for protection.

Though he was operating near an urban center, the vigilant Ah San largely avoided the city and had always managed to stay one step ahead of the authorities. Then Hendropriyono caught a break: Ah San's wife had been on the receiving end of a forced marriage; she was still in love with a lower-ranking guerrilla that An San had conveniently assigned to a different sector.

By luck, Hailintar captured the spurned lover, who in turn discretely led them to Ah San's wife. Both proved amenable to becoming informants, provided they occasionally got to spend time with each other at a Kopassandha safe house.

Even with the leads offered by this pair, Ah San was hard to pin down. Finally, after six months of patient surveillance, Halilintar had narrowed down Ah San's likely location to a remote village. On 3 December 1973, Hendropriono joined his team as they stealthily approached the village in question for what he hoped was their biggest capture to date. Emphasizing the need to take their target alive, he kept his AK-47 strapped to his back and wielded only a knife in his hands.

Working their way through the foliage, Halilintar reached the village perimeter. But Ah San kept multiple guard dogs for just such an occasion, and the hounds picked up the scent of trespassers and began to bay.

Losing the element of surprise, Halilintar rushed forward. Sprinting in the lead, a Kopassandha corporal kicked in the door of the hut believed to be Ah San's residence. Hendropriyono was only a step behind, vaulting through a window. The barking dogs, however, had given sufficient forewarning to Ah San. Wielding a bayonet affixed to an antiquated rifle, the guerrilla sliced open the corporal's stomach. Turning on Hendropriyono, he stabbed the captain in his left thigh, left bicep, and right hand. Reaching for his pistol with severely lacerated fingers, Hendropriyono managed to fire off one fatal round before collapsing in a pool of his own blood.

It was just over two years later when Hendropriyono arrived in Suai to link up with Nanggala 8, and jagged scars were still plainly visible across his hand and arm. By the time he moved with Nanggala 8 to Dili, he had already reached some early, uncomfortable conclusions about the unfolding counter-insurgency campaign in Timor:

There was no finesse. It was all brute strength: columns of infantry, with armor alongside. The Timorese were only being used as coolies, as servants. When I got to Dili, I made it a point to meet the locals. In one family, the siblings went to four different political parties. This was not just a civil war. It was an intra-family war. How could we understand these nuances? Only the Timorese could.[13]

Sensing these critical deficiencies, Hendropriyono was eager to implement some of the lessons learned in West Kalimantan. Soon he got that chance. As Nanggala 8 was exceedingly top-heavy with officers, several were rotated back to Java prior to the conclusion of the tour. Shortly after shifting to Dili, Lieutenant Colonel Soekiman's intelligence assistant, Johannes Moeryono, was among those given a new assignment; Hendropriyono was tapped to take his place.[14]

In this new slot, one of the first things Hendropriyono did was to start learning the local tongue, Tetum. An Austronesian language spoken across Timor, Tetum came in four dialects; the dialect most commonly used around Dili and its environs, appropriately known as Tetum Dili, contained about 20 percent of its vocabulary borrowed from Portuguese. As there were no qualified Tetum tutors readily available, Hendopriyono had to improvise:

> I walked into a church in Dili and found a book among the pews called *Santíssima Trindade*, "The Holy Trinity." It had phrases in both Tetum and Portuguese, so I took it back and started going through it slowly, adding to my vocabulary each day.[15]

Hendropriyono also began to spend as much time as possible among the Timorese, working his way up the food chain to the nascent crop of leaders drawn from Apodeti and UDT. "I did this, and spent the time learning Tetum," he recalled, "because I instinctively knew I would be coming back to Timor."

Meantime, the politico-military landscape in Timor was fast changing. On 17 July, East Timor was officially integrated as an Indonesian province. Two weeks later on 1 August, Kogasgab was renamed the Regional Security and Defense Command (*Komando Daerah Pertahanan dan Keamanan*, or Kodahankam) for what was now termed "stabilization" operations in East Timor. Command of Kodahankam went to newly-promoted Brigadier General Dading Kalbuadi. A Kopassandha alumnus, Dading arguably had more Timor experience than any other member of the Indonesian Armed Forces. He had served in the Timor theatre uninterrupted for more than a year, first as head of the Flamboyan operation, then as the intelligence assistant under Kogasgab.

Now as head of Kodahankam, Dading managed an ongoing deployment

---

13   Interview with A.M. Hendropriyono, 1 May 2000.
14   One of the officers returning early was prayudha commander Subagyo, who rotated back to Jakarta in August to become one of President Suharto's personal bodyguards. Subagyo H.S. interview.
15   Two years later, Hendropriyono wrote a primer on the Tetum language for *Baret Merah*, the monthly Kopassandha journal. *Baret Merah* (May 1978, No. 18), p. 25.

of about 15,000 Indonesian soldiers, police, marines, and airmen. East Timor itself was divided into three sectors—East, Central, and West—each of which was allocated a Regimental Combat Team headed by an army colonel.

As before, Kopassandha continued to play a significant role in stabilization operations. Nanggala 10, which consisted of a para-commando company with a large number of fresh young officers, had already arrived during the second quarter of 1976 and was posted to the central sector.[16] In addition, General Yogie on 20 July ordered replacements be prepared to swap out Nanggala 8, which was set to conclude its tour by the opening of August. Because Nanggala 8 was deemed too large and unwieldy, the replacements were to be divided into two smaller, more manageable entries: Nanggala 11, consisting of a *karsa yudha*, and Nanggala 12, comprising a para-commando company.

By the close of July, both Nanggala 11 and 12 were airlifted into Timor and posted to the western sector. All the elements of Nanggala 8, in turn, assembled in Dili to await a Pelni ship to take them back to Surabaya. As it turned out, however, no Pelni ships were readily available; for the time being, their return to Java was put on hold.

While Nanggala 8 sulked in Dili at their bad fortune, the delay proved fortuitous to Hendropriyono. He remained busy expanding his contacts among the upper strata of Timorese society, culminating in a meeting on 10 August with arguably the four most prominent Timorese in the new provincial government. The first was Arnaldo dos Reis de Araujo, the Apodeti leader and chief of the PGET who a week earlier was officially inaugurated as the East Timor governor. The second was Mario Sanches da Costa, a former Fretilin member who had defected to the PGET and was named district chief for Dili. The third, Francisco Lopes da Cruz, was a one-time seminarian who, transferring to the military and serving a combat tour in Mozambique, became one of the highest-ranking Timorese officers in the Portuguese colonial army. Returning to Timor, he then led the UDT political party and the previous week was named the East Timor deputy governor.[17]

The fourth, 29-year old Abilio Osorio Soares, was head of public works in the East Timor provincial government. His grandfather had been a member of the traditional ruling class in the central town of Laklubar, which had yielded the Osorio Soares family considerable land and status in that vicinity. But it was the family's advocacy of close ties to Indonesia that had rocketed

---

16 Nanggala 9, consisting of a karsa yudha, was posted to Papua to replace Nanggala 1.
17 Lopes da Cruz served in Mozambique from 1968-1970, then returned to Timor and was assigned to the military training center. He left the military in 1973 with the rank of captain. Lopes da Cruz interview.

them to prominence over the past decade. In fact, his eldest brother, Jose, had founded Apodeti and was the party's secretary general at the time of Portugal's departure.

As it turned out, the family's tight embrace of Indonesia had also caused them intense suffering. Among Abilio's thirteen siblings, an older brother, Manuel Vladimirio Osorio Soares, had been caught in 1965 having an affair with a member of the Indonesian consulate in Dili. As punishment, he was reverse-exiled to Portugal and never allowed to return.

Eldest sibling Jose met a more tragic fate. As the smallest of the three main Timorese political parties, Apodeti had attempted to remain on the sidelines during the August 1975 UDT coup and subsequent Fretilin counter-putsch. But as the situation in Dili grew untenable during September, most Apodeti members headed for the West Timor border. Jose was an exception to the rule, defiantly remaining in Dili amid the growing tension. He perhaps felt safe because Apodeti had not taken up arms in the capital and was thus not a direct military challenge to Fretilin. Too, Jose in 1955 had been a seminarian in Macao along with Francisco Xavier de Amaral, the Fretilin president. What's more, Amaral had married Jose's younger sister Lucia; it is likely he felt his brother-in-law would shield him from Fretilin excesses.

For a time, he was right. But Fretilin's patience wore thin by 5 October, when Jose's car was stopped at a Dili checkpoint and he was bundled off to detention in the town's small museum. By the time of the Seroja invasion, he and hundreds of other Apodeti and UDT prisoners—many required to carry boxes of ammunition—were forcibly marched south into the jungle with the retreating Falintil. By year's end, he was being jailed in an underground cell in the town of Same. Then on the night of 27 January 1976, as Indonesian infantry were converging on Same—motivated, ironically, by the threat of the Winspeare delegation visiting the town—Fretilin guards took him out of his cell and put a bullet in his head.[18]

Abilio's younger brother Domingos Osorio Soares, a teenager at the time, had been imprisoned and forced to kneel alongside Jose on that fateful night. He, too, was executed.

Meantime, Domingos Pinto Soares, who was married to Abilio's elder sister Elsa, also had a top position in Apodeti. By day he worked in the customs office along with Fretilin's Francisco Xavier de Amaral. But again, the familial ties with Amaral ultimately counted for little. Taken prisoner in Dili

---

18 Hendro Subroto, *Eyewitness to Integration of East Timor* (Jakarta: Pustaka Sinar Harapan, 1997), p. 53.

during October, Domingos was taken in chains to Aileu in early December. As Indonesian troops were on the verge of seizing Aileu at year's end, he was executed in retaliation.

Abilio, then, had lost two brothers and a brother-in-law to Fretilin within the past eight months. His hatred of the pro-independence party was beyond question.

Hendropriyono sat across from Abilio during their meeting of 10 August, and was familiar with the suffering his family had enduring. Speaking in a slow mix of English, Indonesian, and Tetum, the captain made his pitch to the four Timorese.

"Can you recommend a Timorese who can lead other Timorese troops with me into battle?" he asked.

Abilio quickly nodded his head. "I have a younger brother. He is the one."

*

The younger brother in question, Francisco Osorio Soares, was tenth among the fourteen Osorio Soares siblings. At eighteen years of age in 1973, he had entered *Tropas* for three years of compulsory service. By the time of the Carnation Revolution, he was a non-commissioned officer within the administrative section based at the *Quartel General* in Dili.

Over the next year, Francisco continued to diligently report to the *Quartel General*. The head of the administrative section, a captain from the Azores, and his deputy, a lieutenant from Lisbon, tried their best to maintain morale as tension among the Timorese political parties edged upward. For the time being, most of the Timorese non-commissioned officers were attempting to remain above the fray, professing their political neutrality. That included Francisco, despite the fact his extended family was closely associated with Apodeti.

Then came the UDT coup of August 1975. Francisco was quickly disarmed by UDT loyalists, but otherwise not harmed. In the confusing aftermath of the coup, he and a squad of his *Tropas* peers were shuttled around central Timor before finally being directed toward Baucau.

By the time Francisco arrived in Baucau, it was apparent UDT was fast losing ground to Fretilin. UDT members soon began shuffling their feet and contemplating ways of fleeing toward the Indonesian border. Meantime, rumors started reaching Baucau about harsh Fretilin retribution being meted out to UDT, and a lesser extent Apodeti, in the countryside.

Over the ensuing month of September, Fretilin attempted to fill the power vacuum in disjointed fashion. Francisco, maintaining a low profile, picked his way through the chaos toward Manatuto district. Manatuto ran like a thick band from the north to south coasts midway across Portuguese Timor. Centered in the mountainous interior of that district were two towns of importance, Laklubar and Soibada.

The first of these, Laklubar, was located in a sub-district of the same name in a small valley surrounded by hills like a horseshoe. The terrain in the area was rugged and thickly forested, punctuated by small springs. There were also small deposits of viscous tar dotting the landscape, which since late the previous century had drawn Europeans looking for petroleum. These European encroachments had rubbed the Laklubar natives raw, who were known for their independent streak.

The second town, Soibada, was also located in a sub-district of the same name. More than just about anywhere in Timor, Soibada was steeped in mysticism. Generations prior to any written record, legend had it that Foho Aitara, a mountain overlooking the town to the northeast, was held sacred by locals. After the Portuguese arrived, the legend took on Catholic overtones: several women were now said to have seen an apparition of the Virgin Mary under a large banyan tree on the summit of the mountain.

Though details about the Marian apparition were fuzzy, the Catholic Church embraced the story. The anniversary of the sighting was set on 16 October—year unknown—prompting Timorese from across the territory to make annual pilgrimages to the site. This, in turn, inspired the Church to make a shrine atop Foho Aitara, and to build a church, convent, and high school within Soibada proper.

The Soibada high school, run by Portuguese and Goan missionaries, took on great significance within Portuguese Timor. With few alternatives for a secondary education, children from prominent families in the vicinity of Laklubar and Soibada were exceedingly fortunate to have such a facility in their immediate neighborhood. Not surprisingly, when the three Timorese political parties took shape, the Soibada graduates passed for local intelligentsia and comprised a disproportionate number of leaders in Fretilin, UDT, and Apodeti.

On a map, Soibada was approximately 15 kilometers south of Laklubar, the two connected by one main dirt road and a series of splinter trails. The Osorio Soares family owned a large estate roughly midway between the two, and it was there that Francisco arrived in late September.

At the time, Fretilin was still busy cementing their control across the territory. Though the Osorio Soares family was unapologetically pro-Apodeti, higher priorities kept Fretilin from getting around to confront them. Francisco thus felt safe to begin weekly treks to Sunday mass at the Church of the Sacred Heart of Jesus in Soibada. While he saw prisoners being escorted by Falintil guards along the way, he himself escaped harassment.

In early October, at around the same time his brother Jose was arrested in Dili, Francisco noticed the mood had darkened. Not by coincidence, clashes with pro-integration forces along the Indonesian border were on the rise. Falintil troops around Laklubar and Soibada, as a result, were increasingly baring their teeth in public. While details were elusive, stories of summary executions rippled through the villages.

All of this put Francisco on edge. When word spread that a large Falintil formation was approaching their estate, he headed for the nearby hills. There the family had built crude accommodations within a shallow cave. Three decades earlier Francisco's mother, who was half Portuguese, had hid there to escape the occupying Japanese, who were known to be harsh toward lighter-skinned Timorese.

For two weeks, Francisco remained sequestered in the cave. Finally judging the situation to be suitably stable, he made his way back home. But informants soon tipped off Falintil; Francisco, as a result, was bundled off in cuffs to Laklubar.

By the time Seroja kicked off in early December, Francisco was still being detained in a locked room in the *Tropas* officer's quarters in Laklubar. Weeks, then months, passed in this fashion. While the Indonesian military was slowly working its way into major urban centers and along the coasts, they had yet to tackle much of the mountainous interior.

In mid-February 1976, there was a stir when elements of the Fretilin Central Committee moved through Laklubar. This included Francisco Xavier de Amaral, who was married to Francisco's sister Lucia (though the two had since separated due to being on opposing sides of the political upheaval). Learning that his younger brother-in-law was in detention, Amaral asked that he be brought forward.

As Francisco appeared, Amaral spoke in sympathetic tones and made a pitch for Francisco to join Falintil. To this, Francisco remained non-committal, claiming he preferred to go home to care for his aging parents.

Angered at the rebuff, Amaral rose to leave. As he was departing, he turned back. In an almost causal fashion, he revealed that Jose had been executed late the previous month. Broken by the news, Francisco was ushered back to his cell.

Another two months after that, the Fretilin Central Committee again began to converge in the vicinity. This time they were planning their first party congress since the Indonesian invasion. It was to be held in May at the Church of the Sacred Heart of Jesus in Soibada.

Arriving a few weeks early to make preparations was Fretilin leader Nicolau Lobato. He was a Soibada native, and the Lobato and Osorio Soares families had been close for generations. Nicolau, in fact, had attended the Soibada high school alongside two of Francisco's siblings.

Hearing of Francisco's incarceration, Nicolau asked that he be transferred down to Soibada. There, in the church's rectory, Nicolau was awaiting Francisco with tears in his eyes. He appeared genuinely sorrowful over the death of Jose, and in this contrite state penned a decree stating Francisco was free to travel back to his family estate.

The subsequent Fretilin congress in Soibada, which lasted from 20 May to 2 June, proved to be a pivotal event in the party's history. The congress had been intended as a forum to discuss the organization of Falintil and the arrangement of sectors and regions in the face of Indonesian occupation. But it quickly devolved into heated debate within the Central Committee, pitting more pragmatic *Tropas* veterans against ideological firebrands. The leftist ideologues emerged victorious, insisting that political commissars take charge of Falintil. This move would not only lead Falintil to adopt harsher tactics against the Indonesians, but also against what it saw as dissent within their own ranks.

Following the congress, Nicolau made a point of pausing at the Osorio Soares estate. Once more, Francisco was asked to join Falintil, this time as a regional commander for Manatuto district. Again, Francisco declined the offer.

Nicolau was visibly saddened by the rejection. The rise of the Fretilin ideologues at the congress, he said, left little room for tolerance. "If you don't join us, you are the enemy," Nicolau warned. "You can't remain neutral in this war."

Two weeks later, as Francisco was butchering a cow on the edge of the estate, two Fretilin emissaries approached with orders to escort him to a Falintil command post in the adjacent hills. It was not clear if he would again face detention, or worse.

Their arrival was not by accident. As Francisco prepared to leave with the emissaries, an Apodeti sympathizer discretely entered the estate and got his attention. The Indonesian military was already massing inside Laklubar, Francisco was told, and was preparing to push south toward Soibada.[19]

---

19 Ahead of the ground operation to seize control of Laklubar, the Indonesian Air Force

Sidestepping the emissaries, Francisco bid farewell to his parents and stole out of the compound. Heading north toward Laklubar, he had barely covered any territory before encountering a cluster of Kopassandha para-commandos. They were from was Nanggala 10, which had been assigned to support the offensive south from Laklubar.

Francisco approached the young officers of Nanggala 10. One of them, Lieutenant Prabowo Subianto, spoke fluent English. Gathering that Francisco was a member of Apodeti and wanted to help, Prabowo directed him toward an infantry company that was following in the wake of the para-commandos.

Francisco soon came upon the infantrymen. They were from Infantry Battalion 123, a unit dispatched to East Timor from North Sumatra. Still sticking to the cover story that the Indonesians in Timor were volunteers, Infantry Battalion 123 was outfitted in plain khaki uniforms devoid of army insignia. They were also outfitted with an assortment of Portuguese weapons that had been seized from *Tropas* armories overlooked by Falintil.

Francisco quickly offered his services to the battalion. The Indonesians by then had belatedly learned of the Fretilin congress in Soibada, and were hoping to catch some Fretilin leaders that might still be lingering in town. But fearing an ambush along the main road to Soibada, the battalion wanted to use secondary trails. Francisco proposed to act as their guide and the column was soon marching south. They arrived at Soibada unopposed, as Fretilin had already melted into the hills.

After entering Soibada, Francisco remained with Infantry Battalion 123 for nearly a month. This provided an opportunity to learn some rudimentary Indonesian. But as with nearly every other Timorese volunteering for the Indonesians, he was relegated to menial tasks.

Disillusioned, on 22 July Francisco took leave of Manatuto district and headed back to Dili after an absence of nearly a year. There he met up with older brother Abilio, who was already working in the provincial government, and his widowed sister Elsa.

On account of his family's close history with Apodeti, it was not long before Francisco was offered a job as head of social affairs under the governor's office. But that, too, was not to his liking. He wanted to exact revenge against Fretilin, but not as a coolie for the Indonesian army.

Just such an opportunity came late on the afternoon of 10 August, when a black sedan pulled in front of Elsa's house. An Indonesian army officer

---

assigned an AC-47 gunship to conduct strikes around the two for two weeks. Interview with Chappy Hakim, 18 July 2016.

knocked on the door and asked for Francisco. Learning his was not at home at the time, the officer departed without leaving his name.

Donning a fresh set of clothes from the wardrobe of the deceased Jose, Francisco the next morning headed to the governor's office. His curiosity piqued, he wanted to track down the officer with the black sedan. As it turned out, Hendropriyono was sitting in the governor's waiting room as he arrived. Using a blend of languages and hand gestures, the captain invited him down the street for lunch.

Over a plate of *nasi goreng*, Hendropriyono thought aloud. He wanted to create a fighting force in which the Timorese would be full-fledged soldiers, not coolies. He saw himself as its deputy commander, with a Timorese in actual charge.

"Do you want to go to war?" he asked. "With me?"

Francisco was emphatic. "Yes!"

Back at Elsa's house that night, Francisco outlined what had transpired during the meeting. But after two days without further contact, Francisco was wondering if the offer had not been serious. Impatient, he returned to the governor's office the next morning to again meet the captain. Trouble was, he could not remember Hendropriyono's name.

Knocking on the door for Governor Araujo, Francisco appealed for help. "I want to see the Indonesian with the scars on his arm."

Very quickly, Hendropriyono was at the office and apologizing for the delay. Realizing his name might be difficult to memorize, he gave Francisco a childhood nickname. "My friends call me Edo."

"My friends call me Iquito," replied Francisco.

"I want a platoon of Timorese, Iquito. You will be commander. I will be your deputy," explained Hendropriyono. "Pick three more leaders, then we make our platoon and go to war."

CHAPTER NINE

RAMAHANA

It took only a day for Francisco to finalize his three picks for fellow Timorese to help lead the platoon. The first of the three, Vidal Sarmento, came from a landed family in Laklubar that had been close to the Osorio Soares clan for generations. Vidal himself was six years older than Francisco and had already completed his compulsory military service by the time of the Carnation Revolution. He had joined Apodeti at the party's outset and was serving as its district secretary for Manatuto when UDT seized power in August 1975.

On the morning of that coup, headstrong UDT sympathizers detained members of Apodeti in Laklubar, including Vidal, and demanded that they change party affiliation. Vidal, along with almost all of the other Apodeti adherents, shrugged their shoulders, feigned loyalty to UDT, and were out of detention within three hours.

Fretilin was not nearly as accommodating. After consolidating control in Laklubar, they swooped into Vidal's house on 11 September and put him in shackles. Marched from Laklubar to Manatuto town, he was lined up against a prison wall on three separate occasions for mock executions. Not even the fact that the father of Nicolau Lobato was Vidal's baptismal godfather spared him this treatment.

And Vidal was hardly alone. By the opening of December, the Manatuto prison (in the former district chief's office) was grossly over-populated with UDT and Apodeti sympathizers. This provided an opportunity on 13 December, when Vidal and 130 of his fellow detainees overwhelmed the small guard force and spilled into the streets. Vidal took pains to sever the phone lines leading from Manatuto, depriving the resident Falintil garrison of their main mode of communication with neighboring towns.[1]

Avoiding roads and trails, Vidal picked his way carefully toward Soibada sub-district. For the next six months, he lived off the land and refrained from visiting any settlements of significance for fear of re-arrest. Not until he saw Indonesian military convoys moving into Soibada town did he risk coming out of hiding. Coming out of the jungle, he cut quite a sight. Among the first to see him was Lieutenant Prabowo Subianto from Nanggala 10:

> He was wearing a sarong, waving an Indonesian flag in one hand, holding a Mauser in the other. And his hair and beard! Not cut for six months! He looked like a real mountain man.[2]

Making his way back to Laklubar, Vidal found Fretilin had razed his house to the ground in retaliation for his December escape. He then ventured across town and was given shelter in one of the houses owned by the Osorio Soares family. He was still there when Francisco placed a call in mid-August and beckoned him to Dili. Between his imprisonment and the destruction of his house, Vidal did not need to be asked twice when Francisco proposed that he take up arms against Falintil.

Francisco's second recruit was Antonio Barbosa de Oliveira. Hailing from Laklubar, Antonio's father had been killed by the Japanese for harboring Australian commandos during World War Two. His older brother Domingos had been a seminarian in Macao along with Fretilin's Amaral and Apodeti's Jose Osorio Soares, then had been a founding member of UDT and was its secretary general at the time of the 1975 coup. Antonio himself had been serving in *Tropas* alongside Francisco when the civil war broke out. Though he himself was not imprisoned, he lost two brothers to Fretilin firing squads.

Francisco's final recruit was Domingos do Espirito Santo. Much like his close friend Antonio, he was a Laklubar native, had been serving in *Tropas* when the civil war started, and came from a family of UDT party members. He had one family member executed by Fretilin.

Including Francisco, all of these initial recruits were from the Laklubar and Soibada vicinity. Obviously, any platoon they helped form would operate in this neighborhood. Before the cart got too far in front of the horse, Hendropriyono on 17 August ventured to Laklubar to get tentative approval for his scheme from the ranking on-scene Indonesian military commanders.[3]

---

1 Vidal interview.
2 Interview with Prabowo Subianto, 9 June 2017.
3 *"Laporan Penugasan Nanggala 13 Kopassandha di Timor-Timur,"* p. 11.

Topping that list was Colonel Ramli Hasan Basri, the head of Regimental Combat Team 13. Stabilization operations in the central sector of East Timor, which included Manatuto district, were the responsibility of this regiment. Basri was allocated four infantry battalions for the job, but they were stretched impossibly thin.

As the captain explained his plan, Basri listened attentively. At a time when Timorese were having their role cut back in the security sector, Hendropriyono wanted to dramatically reverse that trend and arm a Timorese platoon to the teeth in order to raise hell in the Manatuto countryside. Even more jolting, Hendropriyono said that he alone—at least initially—would provide the only oversight.

A smile spread across Basri's face. Though it sounded like the captain had a death wish, he did not want to be the one to stifle unorthodox thinking on the part of a junior officer. Basri offered no opposition.

Next, Hendropriyono visited Major Mulyadi, the commander of Infantry Battalion 123. The same battalion that Francisco had assisted for a month, they were still split among a series of outposts around Laklubar. Like Basri, Mulyadi harbored no objections if the captain wanted to take the fight to Fretilin.

Heading back to Dili, Hendropriyono now had to argue his case with the head of Kodahankam, Brigadier General Dading Kalbuadi. The captain had reason for optimism: Dading had been his group commander when first joined Kopassandha.[4]

As it turned out, Dading was not such an easy sell. Recalls Hendropriyono:

> I told him that the ranking Portuguese officer in Timor for a long time was only a major. They were able to do this because they kept the traditional leaders in place, just like the Dutch did in Jogjakarta and Solo. I asked why was Dading a brigadier general? It was because we were not keeping the traditional Timorese leadership in place. I told him that if we applied some of my strategies, we only needed two years to pacify the province. For the moment, I wanted to raise a Timorese platoon; if it was a success, I wanted to bring in a single *prayudha* to help.[5]

When Hendroprioyono was finished with his pitch, Dading was dismissive. "Too much theory," he chided.

Still, Nanggala 8 had finished its tour and was ready to return to Java as soon as a ship became available. If Hendropriyono was eager to remain for another tour, Dading did not want to discourage such enthusiasm. He wrote a letter of recommendation, but insisted that he go back to Jakarta and get

---

4   Hendropriyono interview.
5   *Ibid.*

permission from the Kopassandha commander.

Making progress, Hendropriyono hopped a flight to Jakarta and was soon sitting in front of General Yogie in Cijantung. After outlining his proposal, he sat back and awaited a response. Yogie was not fully convinced, remembered Hendropriyono:

> He saw the risk of losing a captain in a very exposed situation. He was not sure I could trust the Timorese. He was being protective of me.[6]

Hendropriyono had a ready reply to assuage Yogie's concerns. "They have historically backed us. One had his brothers assassinated by Fretilin. They want revenge."

Yogie was silent for a moment, then relented. He would permit Hendropriyono to remain in East Timor to make his platoon and get some initial results. If those initial results were positive, Yogie would consider sending a *prayudha* to assist.

As he was already in Jakarta, Hendropriyono ventured downtown to visit the military's intelligence chief, Major General Benny Moerdani. The two had met on one previous occasion, immediately after Hendropriyono's second tour in West Kalimantan. On that occasion, Benny had praised his efforts.

Listening to Hendropriyono's current plan to raise an indigenous platoon, Benny offered some measured words of advice:

> You had experience and success in Kalimantan. But it is different in Timor and you must be careful. In Kalimantan, you encountered guerrilla forces. In Timor, you fill fight a guerrilla army. They are a conventional army that is now conducting guerrilla warfare. It is much, much harder.[7]

Though he did not want to argue the point, Hendropriyono felt the Falintil guerrilla threat was perhaps over-stated. During conversations with Francisco and Vidal before heading to Jakarta, he was left with the impression that Falintil—with its strong ties to *Tropas*—was not a perfect reflection of Mao's dictum about guerrilla fish swimming in a sea of people:

> When I was in Kalimantan, the guerrillas were one with the people. But *Tropas* was different, they were not one with the people. The Portuguese officers would never dance with the locals. They might dance with Portuguese girls, or maybe even a mestizo. But never a local Timorese, who they considered 'dirty.'
>
> Then there were roads near the *Tropas* headquarters that were off limits for Timorese to walk down. Only Portuguese could walk down those roads. Iquito

---

6 Ibid.
7 Ibid.

complained about this.

Even the simple act of eating and smoking together with the Timorese. Iquito said the Portuguese wouldn't do it, but the Indonesians would. This made me hopeful.[8]

By the final week of August, Hendropriyono was back in Dili with all of his necessary approvals. In the interim, Francisco and Vidal had been busy assembling recruits in Laklubar. As Laklubar and Soibada were UDT party strongholds, it came as no surprise that many were UDT members. This included a hardnosed former *Tropas* corporal with a touch of Chinese blood named Zeka Vong. Another was Belarmino Lopes da Cruz, the younger brother of UDT party leader Francisco Xavier Lopes da Cruz. A former military policeman, Belarmino was angling for revenge after being publicly humiliated in September 1975 when Fretilin consolidated control over Dili.[9]

There were even a handful that came from families with strong Fretilin connections. This included Felix Bertu, a former cattle shepherd in Soibada who had been exempt from *Tropas* service on account of his short stature.[10]

In total, Francisco made a final selection of forty members divided into four squads. As their leader, he was dubbed *comandante*, or commander. True to his promise, Hendropriyono relegated himself to the position of *secunda comandante*, or deputy commander. Their unit was dubbed *Peloton Khusus*, or the Special Platoon.

Though special in name, the platoon caught no breaks when it came to obtaining weaponry. Kodahankam's chief of intelligence, Colonel Johnny Sinaga, had managed to scrounge up twenty-seven Mausers from captured *Tropas* stores, but just ten of these were in good condition. He also provided one ex-Portuguese 60mm mortar with a limited number of rounds, as well as a dated German MG 34 machinegun. Pre-dating World War Two, the MG 34 was considered the world's first general-purpose machinegun. Mercifully from a logistics point of view, it used an ammunition belt with the same caliber bullet as the Mauser. The only equipment allocated from Kopassandha stocks were four PRC-77 tactical radios.[11]

As the platoon assembled for Hendropriyono on a soccer field in Laklubar, they exuded a motley vibe. Their uniforms ranged from *Tropas* fatigues to denim to sports jerseys. Their headgear included baseball caps, berets, and cowboy hats, while footwear was everything from proper combat boots to sandals.

---

8   *Ibid.*
9   Belarmino later married Zeka Vong's sister.
10 Vidal interview.
11 Francisco interview.

Looking them over, Hendropriyono insisted that they partake in some training. To this Francisco protested, insisting that the bulk had already seen service with *Tropas* and were well versed in the tactics and marksmanship. A compromise was reached, whereby the platoon conducted just two days of self-defense drills. On 2 September, they were declared mission-ready.

Now came time to test them in the field. So as not to overwhelm them on their very first operation, Hendropriyono conjured a relatively easy trial run. He did not have to look far, as Falintil was lurking in the hills just outside the Laklubar town perimeter. One concentration was said to be in village of Manelima, 2 kilometers to the south. Though still woefully short of firearms, the platoon duly marched into the hills at daybreak, approaching Manelima with a minimum of noise. Francisco had remained behind in Laklubar next to Hendropriyono; the former had implored the latter not to join the raid. "If Edo got killed on that first mission," the *comandante* recalled, "our project would have come to an immediate end." [12]

Reaching the outskirts of Manelima, the platoon rushed the village with guns blazing. The resident Falintil cell had been on the watch for a plodding Indonesian infantry advance, not a nimble attack by fellow Timorese. They paid for their complacency dearly: when the dust settled, thirteen Falintil guerrillas lay dead. What's more, the platoon was able to collect three Getme rifles, two Mausers, and five grenades left behind.

The raid had not been without cost, however. One member of the platoon, Gaspar, had been captured by the retreating Failintil. Word later got back to Laklubar that he was executed in reprisal.

When the platoon returned to base at day's end, there was relief all around. His concept vindicated, Hendropriyono fired off a message to Dili lauding their first outing. Francisco was somewhat less elated: after getting word that Antonio Barbosa de Oliveira had been overly passive during the attack, he was quietly relegated to a logistics slot. In his place, Zeka Vong was moved up the chain of command.[13]

Word of their success quickly made the rounds of Laklubar sub-district. Within a few days dozens of new recruits materialized, swelling the size of the platoon to eighty men. This further strained logistics; even the best efforts of Hendropriyono had only managed to secure one firearm for every other man.[14]

For the platoon's next mission, the stakes grew exponentially. Over the

---

12   *Ibid.*
13   *Ibid.*
14   "*Laporan Penugasan Nanggala 13 Kopassandha di Timor-Timur,*" p. 14.

previous year, a cult following had developed around Failintil field commander Leonardo da Costa Alves. A native of Ossu sub-district, Alves in his late teens had briefly worked as an elementary school teacher in Liquica district, just west of Dili. He had then been called up for mandatory military service at age 18, joining *Tropas* in the same batch as Francisco Osorio Soares. Alves proved to be an unassuming recruit, though he raised eyebrows among his fellow soldiers for his unusually high voice and effeminate mannerisms.

Then came the UDT coup of August 1975. Alves was quick to join Falintil and underwent a remarkable transformation. "I saw him in late August behind the wheel of a jeep in Dili," recalled one Fretilin colleague. "He had a rifle propped on the hood of the jeep, a military cap pulled down low over his head, and looked just like a general." [15]

Taking leave of Dili, Alves took it upon himself to recruit a guerrilla band of some 200 Fretilin supporters. Like himself, all of his recruits came from the easternmost districts. By September 1975, Alves had led his guerrillas west into Liquica district. There, at least initially, he won grassroots support by enacting deadly revenge against a wealthy UDT family charged with sexual abuse against village girls and forced labor on their coffee plantation.

Very quickly, however, Alves began what could only be described as a scorched earth policy across the Liquica countryside. Left behind was a trail of rapes and robberies, irrespective of party affiliation. [16]

As his excesses began to mount, the Seroja invasion took place and Alves was able to re-focus his guerrillas. Setting up ambushes against the road-bound Indonesians, he put his own unique spin on the strategy using a tactic dubbed *Ramahana*, Tetum for "Bow and Arrow." This involved a small number of guerrillas firing off rounds as bait, then luring the Indonesian troops toward the main body of guerrillas arranged in a killing zone. Alves became so synonymous with this strategy that he adopted Ramahana as his nom de guerre.

In April 1976, *Comandante* Ramahana saw his biggest success to date. As a truck convoy with members of the Brigade 4 headed south from Aileu township, his guerrillas struck. The brigade's official history admits 33 troops were killed in this single engagement; brigade veterans put the actual death toll at 52. In addition, Ramahana made off with dozens of firearms and a

---

15 Alberto X.P. Carlos interview.
16 Douglas Anton Kammen, *Three Centuries of Conflict in East Timor* (New Jersey: Rutgers University Press, 2015), pp. 126-131. Francisco Osorio Soares, who remembered Ramahana as a sociable *Tropas* colleague, was especially shocked by Ramahana's sadistic proclivities after August 1975. Francisco interview.

tactical radio.[17]

After that, Ramahana's reputation went from strength to strength. Falintil lauded his efforts, giving him credit for a string of further ambushes. One story, possibly apocryphal, claimed he leapt aboard an Indonesian tank and dropped a grenade down the open hatch, killing the crew. Adding to his mystique, he wore a necklace choked with wooden amulets; these were said to make his body impervious to bullets, even if they riddled his clothes.[18]

Then in mid-September, word reached Laklubar that Ramahana and his so-called Failintil Special Forces were moving into the vicinity. Coincidentally, the Indonesian government had earlier prepared 10 tons of rice to be distributed among the peasantry in Manatuto district. In a shrewd move, the Special Platoon was tasked with helping distribute the rice, which greatly assisted them in winning grassroots support. This goodwill had resulted in the initial reports from the peasantry that Ramahana had entered the sub-district.[19]

Hearing the news, Hendropriyono huddled with his senior platoon officers. "He was concerned about us being outnumbered," said Francisco. "Ramahana was supposed to have around 200 soldiers; we were just 40." [20]

Still, Ramahana and his men were outsiders from the eastern districts. The Special Platoon, by contrast, were all natives from Laklubar and Soibada. "It was our home turf," declared Francisco.

In rapid succession, multiple sources helped pinpoint the exact location of Ramahana—and it was uncomfortably close. Two cousins of squad leader Domingos do Espirito Santo reported that the Falintil comandante had bivouacked at Funar, an abandoned hilltop village about 3 kilometers northwest of Laklubar. A third source—a former *Secunda Lina* militiaman from Funar named Rosendo, who was eager to join the Special Platoon—claimed a recent sighting and offered to guide them to their target. Adding further confirmation, the platoon intercepted radio transmissions coming from the Funar vicinity in Ramahana's trademark falsetto.

Eager to go toe-to-toe with the elite Falintil unit, the Special Platoon looked to give Ramahana a taste of his own tactics. Armed with rifles, one mortar, and one machinegun, the platoon divided into squads and, with

---

17 The higher casualty figure, based on veteran interviews, was reported in the 13 September 1999 edition of the Semarang newspaper *Koran Wawasan*.
18 Vidal interview.
19 Francisco interview. Vidal Sarmento later picked up hearsay from Fretilin sources that Ramahana had been dispatched to Laklubar by Nicolau Lobato specifically to track down and attack the Special Platoon. Vidal interview.
20 Francisco interview.

Rosendo in the lead, on 23 September scaled the rugged terrain to take up ambush positions around Funar. From his vantage position to the west, squad leader Domingos could discern no movement. But on the eastern flank, squad leader Zeka Vong could see the Funar hilltop crawling with Falintil.

Down at Laklubar, Hendropriyono was coordinating the raid with elements of Infantry Battalion 123. Relaying coordinates of the Falintil position to the battalion's mortar crew, a string of rounds were sent flying toward Funar.

Predictably, Ramahana and his men scattered to avoid the incoming mortars. As they did, the Special Platoon unleashed repeated volleys from its blocking positions. Not until three hours later, after registering no further return fire, did the platoon cautiously move forward.

Hendropriyono was doing his best to follow developments over his PRC-77. This proved a challenge as the Timorese—adrenaline pumping—were yelling over their radios in their native tongue. Finally at noon, he received a critical update in a mix of Tetum and Portuguese.

"Paneleiro mate ona!" *The homosexual is dead!*

Hendropriyono asked for clarification. They had captured one Getme and three Mausers, radioed back Vidal Sarmento. And they had killed one Falintil: Comandante Ramahana.

That the platoon had managed to kill just one member of the Falintil Special Forces, and that one member happened to be Ramahana, strained credulity. Hendropriyono found himself hard pressed to believe their extraordinary luck.

Up on Funar, meantime, the entire Special Platoon had converged around the Falintil corpse. A couple of *Tropas* veterans who had overlapped with Ramahana at Taibessi a year earlier vouched for his identity. Back at Laklubar, however, doubts persisted. Not interested in withdrawing down the steep slopes while lugging a body, Vidal Sarmento resorted to the extreme:

> We decided to bring back the head so Edo would believe us. Nobody wanted to cut it off, so I ordered one of my juniors to do it. We stuck the head in a rice pouch, buried the rest of the body, and reached Laklubar late in the afternoon.[21]

Presented with the rice pouch, Hendropriyono did his best to suppress shock. A chopper flew in near last light with Colonel Sinaga and a Timorese assistant, who verified Ramahana's identity and took photographs. It was now official: the Special Platoon was the first to kill a senior Falintil commander in the field.[22]

---

21   Vidal interview.
22   Falintil sources later spread a story, with considerable embellishment, that Ramahana was

Two days later, General Dading arrived in Laklubar by chopper to lavish praise on the platoon. At the same time this was transpiring, a Pelni ship had belatedly arrived off of Dili, collected Nanggala 8, and set sail for Surabaya. All of its members were back at Magelang and Cijantung by week's end.[23]

Remaining behind in East Timor, Hendropriyono now had Dading's full blessing to ramp up operations. Only this time, he would be getting help from an entire *prayudha*.

---

killed while valiantly leading a charge while mounted on a white horse. Alberto X.P. Carlos interview.
23   Umpusingga interview.

CHAPTER TEN

THE DIRTY DOZEN

In the wake of the successful mission that killed Ramahana, the platoon immediately engaged in four further skirmishes in the hills around Laklubar. The results were decidedly in their favor: over the course of three weeks through mid-October, they managed to kill a dozen Falintil and capture two Getme rifles, eight Mausers, and twelve grenades. All of this was at the cost of just one wounded platoon member.[1]

Just as significant, on 10 October the platoon received hearsay information that a Falintil guerrilla named Diogo Munis had been executed by fellow Fretilin members because they suspected he betrayed the location of Ramahana.[2] In this particular case, their suspicions were unfounded.

Shortly thereafter, Hendropriyono headed back to Cijantung. Given the progress with the Special Platoon to date, he intended to remind General Yogie of his promise to consider sending a *prayudha* to support his efforts. When they subsequently met, Yogie was not only agreeable, but he gave Hendropriyono leeway to pick his own men.

This was easier said than done. Looking over the available assets within Group 4, Hendropriyono found few men to spare due to the group's heavy counter-insurgency commitments. A large number of them had been assigned to Nanggala 8 (including himself), but they were enjoying downtime after having just returned to base a couple of weeks earlier. Among the only troops on hand came from the former members of Nanggala 2, who had been on the maiden Kopassandha deployment to Timor a year earlier. This nanggala came with a controversial backstory, however. In October 1975, they had been

---
1 "*Laporan Penugasan Nanggala 13 Kopassandha di Timor-Timur*," p. 14.
2 *Ibid.*, p. 17.

assigned to spearhead a raid 10 kilometers across the Timor border against the hilltop town of Balibo. Because Falintil had a substantial presence in that town, and an imminent clash with the Indonesians seemed likely, a five-man television crew (two Australians, two Britons, and one New Zealander) had already taken up residence to film events near the frontline.[3]

As predicted, Nanggala 2, accompanied by a large contingent of Apodeti and UDT partisans, marched toward Balibo on 16 October. With Nanggala 2 strung out along the bottom of the slope firing upward, the nanggala commander, Major Yunus Yosfiah, was giving radio updates to the Flamboyan commander, Colonel Dading, who had edged his forward headquarters across the border to the town of Mota'ain. Lieutenant Gatot Purwanto, Nanggala 2's operations officer, recounted what came next:

> There was a lot of incoming fire raining down from the top of the hill. The Indonesian navy was supposed to help us with gunfire support. While we were on the slope, an incoming round came in from the navy. But it hit really close to us. Major Yunus was on the radio at the time with Colonel Dading at Mota'ain. When the naval round hit, Yunus flinched and rolled one way, and the radioman rolled the opposite direction. The cord to the radio handset snapped, and we lost contact with Dading. Dading was still waiting for permission from his superiors for what we should do next. Without being able to talk to him, [Nanggala 2] went ahead with the attack.[4]

By the time Nanggala 2 and the partisans swarmed across the top of the hill and the dust settled, the five foreign journalists lay dead under cloudy circumstances. This quickly became an international incident, thrusting Indonesia under a critical spotlight. "Dading was pretty furious with Yunus," recalled Gatot. "Most of us were sent back to Cijantung to let things 'cool down.'"[5]

Among those still biding his time at the Group 4 headquarters was Lieutenant Gatot. As it turned out, Gatot and Hendropriyono knew each other from the Task Force 42 days in West Kalimantan. A member of the Military Academy Class of 1971, Gatot was one of a handful of signals officers who went through the commando course and was admitted into Kopassandha. When Hendorpriyono offered him a chance to act as his deputy advising the Special Platoon, he agreed without hesitation.

Next, Hendropriyono went about selecting another dozen Group 4 members to flesh out a full *prayudha*. "Several of them were formerly with [Nanggala 2] and were known as disciplinary cases who were hard to handle,"

---

3   Nanggala 2 was also known by the nickname Team Susi.
4   Interview with Gatot Purwanto, 4 April 2017.
5   *Ibid.*

said Gatot. "But *Pak* Hendro prided himself in giving subordinates a second chance to prove themselves." [6]

Too, Hendropriyono made clear to all prospects that he was intent on practicing true unconventional warfare doctrine:

> I wanted twelve *sandi yudha* members who were not interested in killing, but in convincing Timorese not to kill. I wanted to ensure they would treat the Timorese with dignity.[7]

By mid-October, the final cut of twelve *prayuda* members was made. Together with Hendropriyono and Gatot, the fourteen of them were dubbed Nanggala 13. Compared to its predecessors—and successors—it would be by far the smallest nanggala ever dispatched to East Timor.

On 20 October, Nanggala 13 boarded a C-130 and arrived in Dili. From there, they transferred to Bell choppers and were ferried into Laklubar to meet the Special Platoon for the first time. Hendropriyono's plan was for the Special Platoon to continue with combat missions as before, but with Nanggala 13 providing more advanced training in subjects like ambushes and sniping, assisting with logistics, tending to their medical concerns, and offering advice as needed while on the move. This mentoring arrangement bore more than a strong resemblance to what U.S. Army Special Forces had been doing a decade earlier alongside the Montagnards in South Vietnam.

Though several from Nanggala 13 had dealt with Apodeti and UDT partisans during their earlier Nanggala 2 deployment, this time they were dealing with their Timorese counterparts as equals rather than coolies. This required a sharp sense of tact, observed Gatot:

> There was a kind of caste system in East Timor. Iquito was blue blood from a prominent family. So was Vidal Sarmento. So we could never get mad at them in front of their men; that would have been disastrous.
>
> We also found that once the Timorese got mad, it was hard to calm them down. With Papuans it was different: Papuans were quick to anger, but there were always ways to calm them down, like drinking with them. Timorese were not like that: they would hold a grudge and not cool down. We had to take this into consideration when working alongside them.[8]

With the arrival of Nanggala 13 also came an injection of weapons. For the first time, Kopassandha provided a handful of AK-47s for the platoon's senior

---

6   Gatot interview.
7   Hendropriyono interview.
8   Gatot interview.

cadre. More Getmes and Mausers were also turned over from captured stores. But even these could not keep pace with the steady flow of recruits arriving at Laklubar. By month's end, the platoon had swelled to 124 men. As this was deemed logistically unsustainable, Nanggala 13 on 10 November informed Francisco that the platoon would need to abide by a ceiling of 60 men for the time being.

Besides strained logistics, the platoon faced another serious challenge. The Indonesian army was not always providing them with timely intelligence, which complicated mission planning. To compensate, Nanggala 13 on 23 October sent two unarmed platoon members into the jungle southwest of Soibada on a reconnaissance mission. Handed this task was Abel Soares, an Apodeti member who had been imprisoned at Manatuto alongside Vidal Sarmento, and Felix Bertu, the former cattle shepherd who came from a family of Fretilin supporters.

Within a day, the mission went sour. Running into a Falintil patrol, their cover story fell apart and both were bundled off to the Fretilin-held village of Fahinehan, west of Soibada. There, after three weeks of brutal interrogation, Felix was able to escape and find his way back to the platoon; Abel, however, was executed. The platoon did not attempt any further unarmed reconnaissance forays.

The lack of intelligence from Indonesian army channels soon became moot, as increased Falintil activity around Soibada inundated the platoon with possible targets. In particular, they became fixated on the tiny village of Maloshun, a two-hour hike along a narrow trail to the southeast. This was the home-village of Nicolau Lobato's wife, and the Fretilin president had reportedly retreated there with his family to establish a field communications center. Of even greater concern—from a symbolic point of view—was that fact Lobato had taken the Virgin Mary statue from the shrine atop Foho Aitara and carried it with him to Maloshun.[9]

Together with Nanggala 13, the Special Platoon carefully picked its way through the jungle to encircle Maloshun. On the morning of 17 November, they blitzed the village, killing four Falintil and capturing one. Lobato and his family were nowhere to be found, but the platoon did manage to seize a GRC-9 tactical radio, a generator, and five field telephones with cable. Just as important, they found the Virgin Mary statue tucked away in a cave. In a procession with the platoon on 18 November, Hendropriyono carried the statue back to Foho Aitara while astride a Timor pony.

---

9   Francisco interview.

Next, Nanggala 13 on 19 November got word that Lobato and his family may have shifted to Manehat, a village tucked deep in the jungle south of Soibada. The following night, the platoon raided this latest target. Again Lobato was missing, but they did manage to capture four and seize two rifles. Two of these prisoners were significant. The first was Tito Martins, a former Apodeti member who had been pressured into joining Fretilin and had risen to deputy political secretary for Laklubar. The second was Joao Bosco Quintao, a top Falintil military advisor. Martins pragmatically pledged loyalty to Indonesia and was soon acting as a guide for Infantry Battalion 123. Quintao, given his relatively senior status, was sent back for interrogation in Dili.[10]

Next, multiple intelligence sources indicated Fretilin was planning a leadership meeting in Fahinehan. This was the same village west of Soibada where Felix Bertu had been held prisoner earlier that month. Figuring they could deal a lethal blow to Fretilin by figuratively decapitating its top echelon, Kodahankam rushed plans for a major raid. This was to include not only elements of two infantry battalions, but all in-theater Kopassandha assets. In addition to Nanggala 13 and the Special Platoon, they flew in Nanggala 11 (which consisted of a *karsa yudha*) and Nanggala 12 (comprised of a para-commando company). The latter two had been operating in the western sector for most of their tour, but for the past month had been in Dili acting as mobile reserves.[11]

Fretilin, it seems, had other plans. Rather than gather for a meeting at Fahinehan, they were instead quietly massing for their own raid on the town of Laklubar. On 21 November, they overran an outlying Indonesian army outpost, killing four soldiers and making off with a PRC-77 radio, an assault rifle, and a Soviet-made DShK heavy machine gun.[12]

Whipsawed by Falintil's surprise move, Nanggala 12 and half of the Special Platoon rushed to Laklubar in an attempt to intercept the Failintil guerrillas with the DShK machinegun. By the time they arrived, however, Falintil and the gun had long since disappeared into the hills.

As all this was transpiring, November gave way to December and the

---

10 Nanggala 13 received information that Januario Lobato, Nicoalu's brother and head of Fretilin's Soibada region, was shot dead at Manehat, though his body was allegedly carried off by retreating Falintil. In fact, Januario had escaped Manehat; he was later killed by Nanggala 15 in September 1977. "Kopassandha Nanggala XV," Lampiran-C (Bidang Operasi), p. 26.
11 "Laporan Khusus Pelaksanaan Tugas Team Nanggala XI Kopassandha," p. 4; "Laporan Kegiatan dan Hasil Operasi Team Nanggala XII," p. 11. In the latter report, Nanggala 13 is referred to as "Team Edo."
12 "Laporan Penugasan Nanggala 13 Kopassandha di Timor-Timur," p. 16.

annual rainy season took hold. This greatly complicated transportation in the region, with the trails between Laklubar and Soibada transformed into ribbons of mud. As the Special Platoon had been keeping a hectic pace for the past three months, Francisco was allowed to head back to Dili to rest and Vidal Sarmento took the opportunity to visit his fiancé. Too, Hendropriyono let his deputy, Lieutenant Gatot, run the next two outings.

The first of these, on 2 December, was a quick skirmish in the village of Wamanas that resulted in four dead Falintil and one captured Mauser.

The second operation, on 12 December, was more costly. Heading south of Soibada toward the village of Tacihatin, the platoon ran headlong into a pair of Failintil guerrillas and engaged in a brief firefight. Rushing forward in pursuit, too late they realized they had been lured into a Ramahana-style ambush pioneered by the late Failintil comandante. As heavy gunfire poured in from their flanks, two platoon members—Louis da Consecao and Adelino Soares—collapsed with fatal wounds.[13]

The platoon, it turned out, had a guardian angel on this mission. Only a few months earlier, the Indonesian Air Force had taken delivery of a dozen North American Rockwell OV-10 light attack aircraft. These slow, rugged workhorses were ideally suited for counter-insurgency and had been used extensively by the U.S. Air Force, Marines, and Navy during the Vietnam War. In addition to rockets, the Indonesians had retrofitted their airframes with 12.7mm Browning machine guns in place of the normal 7.62mm guns.

Over Tacihatin that day, a lone OV-10 was cutting a slow orbit. Using a PRC-77 radio wedged near his feet, the co-pilot in the rear seat was trying to maintain voice communication with the platoon below. This was done with varying levels of success, due in no small part to the language barrier between him and the platoon. As the OV-10 came uncomfortably close during one of its strafing runs, Vidal Sarmento struggled to express himself in Indonesian, "Itu kami!" *That's us!* [14]

In the end, the platoon managed to work its way into Tacihatin. Inside they found the corpse of Jose Berlelas, a local Falintil commander. Just as important, a deserter named Silverio came forward and revealed that the platoon had preempted a Falintil attack on Soibada scheduled for the next day; Berlelas was to have been in charge.

Though counting themselves fortunate to have averted an attack on Soibada, Hendropriyono was just getting started. In recent weeks he had

---

13   Gatot interview.
14   *Ibid;* "Laporan Penugasan Nanggala 13 Kopassandha di Timor-Timur," p. 24.

grown increasingly aware of dissent within Falintil ranks. This dated back to the Fretilin congress in Soibada, when the party had divided East Timor into six administrative sectors (roughly analogous to districts), which in turn were split into regions (analogous to sub-districts) and zones (equal to hamlets). Hardline Fretilin revolutionaries at the congress had insisted that political commissars oversee military leaders at all these levels.

Not surprisingly, Falintil's military leadership howled at being subordinated to ideologues. Hendropriyono intended to exploit this gap and stoke suspicions on both sides of the divide, thereby letting Fretilin begin to consume itself. This was not his first such attempt at psychological warfare. "*Pak* Hendro had conducted psychological operations in Kalimantan against the Chinese guerrillas, and they were an incredibly crafty," recalled a fellow Indonesian officer. "By comparison, the Timorese were amateurs." [15]

The first mental bullet in this psychological campaign was fired on 2 December. After the Special Platoon entered Wamanas village, they singled out a suspected Fretilin sympathizer, handed him a sealed envelope, and told him to ensure it was delivered to Nicolau Lobato. In it, a letter warned Lobato of unspecified dangers from within Fretilin's own ranks. The platoon never knew if Lobato got the envelope. But in the event he did, it was an easy way of increasing his paranoia. Moreover, all messages to and from Fretilin officers were routinely vetted by the Central Committee, and that might cause some in the committee to suspect Lobato was secretly in touch with the Indonesians.

The second mental bullet was fired after the Special Platoon overran Tacihatin. Exploiting newfound information—that the deceased Jose Berlelas was supposed to have led an attack on Soibada—they targeted a mid-ranking guerrilla named Matheus, who reportedly headed the Falintil cell in a village just northwest of Soibada. A letter in Tetum was composed as follows:

Matheus,

Thank you for the information. Give the corpse of Jose Berlelas to those who say they want to attack Soibada. Hurry up and run back here before the secret leaks.

Your brother,

Singha

As before, the letter was put in a sealed envelope and handed to a villager with instructions to ensure it was delivered to Matheus. Of course, Matheus had no

---

15 Subagyo H.S. interview.

contact with the Special Platoon, and certainly had not passed any information to the Indonesians. But when the Central Committee vetted the letter, the insinuation would be that Matheus had conspired to spoil the Soibada attack.

In this particular case, the letter had its desired effect: weeks later, the platoon received information that Matheus had been executed on 28 December.[16]

The black letter-writing campaign continued. One, written in gibberish code, was addressed to Jose da Silva. This former *Tropas* sergeant had become the head of the very first Falintil company formed in August 1975. Rising quickly through the ranks, he became Falintil deputy chief-of-staff within a year. But following the Soibada congress, da Silva steadfastly refused the order to let civilian ideologues override military leaders.

As it turned out, the black letter targeting da Silva was largely superfluous: he staged a short-lived rebellion on his own, taking several fellow Fretilin members hostage. He was subsequently arrested and executed by Falintil.[17]

Another black letter, again written in a gibberish code, was addressed to Falintil's chief-of-staff, Guido Soares. As with the da Silva letter, it was meant to make the Central Committee question his true loyalties.[18]

One final black letter was placed in a pair of pants and abandoned along a riverbank north of Soibada. It was addressed to Hermenegildo Alves, a former *Tropas* soldier who had been named Fretilin's deputy defense minister back in November 1975. Though the Special Platoon later received information that Alves had reportedly fallen under a cloud of suspicion, the black letter campaign had ran its course. "It was successful in the beginning," observed Lieutenant Gatot, "but eventually Fretilin caught on." [19]

But by the time Fretilin got wise to the letters, they were largely unnecessary. In August 1977, festering divisions within the Central Committee prompted them to start a widespread witch hunt for suspected traitors. The most senior victim of this crackdown was none other than former Fretilin president Xavier do Amaral—Francisco's brother-in-law—who was arrested for high treason. Ironically, one of the charges leveled against Amaral was his supposed involvement in the death of Comandante Ramahana.[20]

---

16 "*Laporan Penugasan Nanggala 13 Kopassandha di Timor-Timur*," p. 17.
17 The Special Platoon received anecdotal information, incorrect in hindsight, that da Silva was executed by Fretilin in December 1976. "*Laporan Penugasan Nanggala 13 Kopassandha di Timor-Timur*," p. 13.
18 At the time Nanggala 13 composed these black letters, they were under the impression that Guido Soares was the Falintil deputy commander and Jose da Silva was the Falintil chief-of-staff. "*Laporan Penugasan Nanggala 13 Kopassandha di Timor-Timur*," p. 6.
19 Gatot interview.
20 *Timor Information Service*, No. 20/21, October 1977.

CHAPTER TEN - THE DIRTY DOZEN

*

In Laklubar, meantime, Infantry Battalion 123 had rotated back to North Sumatra and was replaced by Infantry Battalion 623 from Kalimantan. Infantry Battalion 123 and its commander had been involved with the Special Platoon since its inception and had been especially supportive. During the raid against Ramahana at Funar, for example, the battalion's mortars had been instrumental. Infantry Battalion 623, however, was spread thin and had neither the men nor the inclination to help with Nanggala 13's unconventional warfare efforts.

To compensate for the lessened infantry support, Nanggala 13 on 15 December was assigned a 23-man para-commando platoon from Group 2. This was led by Warrant Officer Mohammad Tukiran, an officer with recent problems. During an East Timor deployment with Nanggala 6, he and his platoon had been charged with insubordination and sent packing back to Magelang. As was his habit, Hendropriyono was willing to give Tukiran and his men a chance at redemption.[21]

With the nearly two-dozen para-commandos came their machineguns, rocket launchers, and light mortars. Placing this added punch alongside the Special Platoon, Nanggala 13 figured that they could begin tackling more ambitious targets. They get their first—and in hindsight, only—chance to put this to the test in early February 1977 when information was received about a Falintil concentration south of Soibada in Fatuberlio sub-district. Initially, two squads of the Special Platoon were dispatched to the vicinity. Once contact was initiated, a para-commando squad arrived as reinforcements. The two elements worked well together despite language barriers, resulting in the deaths of four Falintil (including a platoon commander using the *nom de guerre* Maunahak).[22]

At the same time, the Special Platoon began dabbling in a different type of operation. Felix Bertu, the cattle shepherd who came from a family of Fretilin sympathizers, led four other platoon members in a team dubbed Commando Five. The plan was for Commando Five to pass themselves off as a Falintil patrol and troll for information, similar to the pseudo-gang strategy later used by the Selous Scouts in Rhodesia. As they would all be armed, they would theoretically be less likely to repeat Bertu's fate of falling prisoner while on a reconnaissance mission back in October.

On 6 January 1977, the team had a test run when it entered the small

---

21 The platoon had fired off all their ammunition into the air following repeated delays to send Nanggala 6 back to Magelang after the conclusion of its tour in East Timor. Gatot interview.
22 "*Laporan Penugasan Nanggala 13 Kopassandha di Timor-Timur*," p. 17.

settlement of Dauloroc, just off the main road between Soibada and Laklubar. But rather than rely on guile, Bertu, who was still smarting from his harsh interrogation at Fretilin hands, had little interest in gathering information. Looking to intimidate, the team left behind three bodies and made off into the jungle.

On 27 January, Commando Five had its second outing. This time, they ventured to Maloshun, the same village southeast of Soibada where Nicolau Lobato had hid the Virgin Mary statue. Again, Bertu appeared to have revenge on his mind as three more bodies were left in their wake. Falling short in its intended reconnaissance mission, the team was subsequently disbanded.

By that time, Nanggala 13 had settled into a familiar routine. The Special Platoon was active in the field, the para-commando platoon was on standby, and the *prayudha* offered oversight from its new quarters in the convent annex at Soibada's Sacred Heart of Jesus Church. There, on the afternoon of 20 February, the *prayudha* was playing volleyball in the field across from the church when they heard sustained gunfire in the hills due north of town. That was the location of an outpost for Infantry Battalion 320, a new unit from Java that had replaced Infantry Battalion 623. Just like its predecessor, Infantry Battalion 320 was spread impossibly thin; just one company was divided among static posts dotting the Soibada sub-district countryside.

Fearing the worst, Nanggala 13 attempted to raise Infantry Battalion 320 on the radio but got no response. Suiting up, the *prayudha* then marched into the hills to investigate. Lieutenant Gatot was on the patrol:

> There was an outpost of 5 men on Manlala Mountain. It was pretty dry up there, so they had gone to a watering hole and stripped down to take a bath. We found five bodies in the water, their heads mounted on bamboo posts. It was gruesome, trying to match up the heads to the bodies. We brought them back to Soibada and, because there were no other options, *Pak* Hendro got permission from the pastor to conduct Islamic rites for them in the church.[23]

Following the Manlala massacre, the Special Platoon consolidated inside Soibada. With one month left to Nanggala 13's scheduled tour, there was only time for a couple of more missions. The last took place on 10 March, when the platoon was supported for a second time by an orbiting OV-10 during a foray north of Soibada.[24]

At month's end, Nanggala 13 concluded its assignment. During the preceding seven months, the Special Platoon had conducted 15 large operations

---

23 Gatot interview.
24 "*Laporan Penugasan Nanggala 13 Kopassandha di Timor-Timur*," p. 24.

and five smaller raids. Combined with the *prayudha* and para-commandos, they had been a potent combination by any appreciable measure. In particular, they had disproportionately inflicted losses on Falintil at the cost of just five platoon members.

For its part, Nanggala 13 itself had suffered no casualties. Even in his highly exposed position prior to the arrival of Nanggala 13, Hendropriyono had emerged unscathed:

> I always got warnings about the Timorese not being reliable, but I never felt threatened. I slept alongside them. I made it a point whenever a rallier with a rifle joined the platoon: the first thing he could do was turn in his rifle for an even better weapon.[25]

Compared to losses suffered by other nanggala, the difference was even more glaring. This was especially true when Kopassandha was misused as light infantry. Case in point was Nanggala 12, which had arrived in Laklubar as reinforcements in November. By the time Nanggala 12 left East Timor in March 1977, ten of its 103 members were dead. That was the highest percent of fatalities suffered by any nanggala to date.[26]

As Nanggala 13 packed to leave, one of its last acts was to nearly double the size of the Special Platoon to 109 men. Francisco remained in charge as *Comandante*, while Vidal Sarmento was promoted to *Secunda Comandante*. Antonio de Oliverira was third in seniority as military advisor. Under them were two zones, Soibada and Laklubar. The Soibada Zone was placed under Zeka Vong. In this zone were two platoons, one led by Felix Bertu and the other by Vidal's cousin, Jose Maria Sarmento. The Laklubar Zone was under Dominggos do Espirito Santo, who doubled as the head of the zone's single platoon.[27]

Morale among the three platoons remained high. Recalled one Laklubar native:

> They would sometimes come to Dili while on leave. They had a real swagger: cowboy hats, red eyes, heavily armed. Belarmino had even gotten his hands on a rocket launcher, and wore it strapped to his back.[28]

---

25 Hendropriyono interview.
26 "*Laporan Kegiatan dan Hasil Operasi Team Nanggala 12*," Lampiran: Kerugian Operasi, p. 1.
27 The company's members were divided on paper into partisans and People's Resistance members (*Perlawanan Rakyat*, or Wanra). The difference: Wanra were formally administered on paper by the Military District Command, while the partisans were administered on a more ad hoc basis. In reality, all members of the company received the exact same equipment and uniforms. Muchdi interview.
28 Alberto X.P. Carlos interview.

The question now became who would inherit the role of supporting them. Nanggala 13 had proven that quality trumped quantity: an exceedingly small unit was up to the task, provided they had the right mindset.

Cijantung, however, did not seem of this opinion. Rather than continuing the trend of smaller, more manageable deployments, the next contingent bound for East Timor, Nanggala 15, was an especially large entity. Arriving on 17 March, it consisted of an understrength para-commando company from Group 1 and a *karsa yudha* from Group 3.[29]

Though big on paper, Nanggala 15 was set to replace Nanggala 11, 12, and 13. As it was to be the only Kopassandha deployment in East Timor for the remainder of 1977, it was expected to cover the entire province with about 65 less troops than the combined total of the three nanggala it was replacing.

In fact, Nanggala 15 could only spare one para-commando platoon for Soibada. There would be no *prayudha* going with them, thus depriving the contingent of more experienced commandos versed in unconventional warfare. And the platoon would only be led by a youthful warrant officer, who would have neither the seniority nor the experience that the officers of Nanggala 13 had provided.

Beginning on 2 April, Puma helicopters ferried the Nanggala 15 platoon to Soibada in four increments. Three days later, Nanggala 13 officially handed over responsibility, turning over control of 57 Getmes and 51 Mausers used by the Special Platoon.

In Dili, Hendropriyono briefed the incoming officers of Nanggala 15. Like himself, there were several veterans from Nanggala 8 among them. The Nanggala 15 commander was Captain Moeryono, his academy classmate who was previously the Nanggala 8 intelligence officer. And one of the *prayudha* commanders was Captain Muchdi, who had led the para-commando company while with Nanggala 8.[30]

But familiar faces aside, Hendropriyono had misgivings his pet project in Soibada would be mismanaged. Months earlier, in fact, he had tried to steer Francisco toward a young lieutenant who seemed to appreciate the nuances of unconventional warfare. Remembers Francisco:

> Edo wanted me to meet with Lieutenant Prabowo Subianto. I had met Prabowo briefly in June [1976] when I first encountered the Indonesian army. He happened to be in the hospital in Dili recovering from a tropical ailment, so I went there to visit him with my

---

29 The preceding nanggala, Nanggala 14, had deployed to Papua in February 1977.
30 Before the Nanggala 15 tour concluded in December 1977, Moeryono was promoted to major and Muchdi was promoted to become its operations officer.

brother Abilio. We hoped that he might be able to take over the Special Platoon after Edo.[31]

Listening to the platoon's accomplishments during its short existence to date, Prabowo was intrigued. An avid reader of military histories, he was well aware of what could be accomplished by a well-led indigenous force. But while he was the son of a cabinet minister, he was just 25 years old and had yet to develop any real sway within Kopassandha. As a result, he could not possibly act on Francisco's offer.

Now with the Special Platoon under the control of Nanggala 15, it did not take long for Hendropriyono's concerns to become a reality.[32] Once settled in Soibada, the para-commando platoon fused with the Timorese inherited from Nanggala 13 and became a full company. Significantly, however, the para-commando platoon commander named himself head of that company.[33] This upended what had made the Special Platoon so unique—the Timorese were no longer in charge. Said Hendropriyono in blunt terms: "They went back to being coolies." [34]

It also became quickly apparent that the Indonesian army intended a far more hardline approach to counter-insurgency in Soibada. The company led by Nanggala 15 began relocating thousands of locals, burning down entire villages in their wake. During just one day in September, 100 huts were torched. On another day in early November, 240 huts were razed and 35 horses seized.[35]

Excesses on that scale were setting a new bar for all the wrong reasons, compounded by the fact that Indonesia's Apodeti and UDT allies were heavily represented among the populous around Soibada. Not surprisingly tension began to rise within the company, with the Timorese souring toward their Kopassandha counterparts. It got so bad that Francisco, who was spending more time in Dili, was beckoned to Soibada to help sooth tempers.[36]

Returning to Dili, Francisco elected to join the provincial government. Similarly, Vidal Sarmento ventured to Jakarta to get training as a sub-district chief; he would ultimately become the Manatuto district chief. Shortly thereafter, the other Timorese who had fought with the Special Platoon went their own way. Several, like Felix Bertu and Belarmino, stayed in the battlefield

---

31 Francisco interview.
32 Hendropriyono returned to Java and in late April was promoted to major and assigned to the staff of Group 2.
33 "*Kopassandha Nanggala XV*," Lampiran-C (Bidang Operasi), pp. 5-6.
34 Hendropriyono interview.
35 "*Kopassandha Nanggala XV*," Lampiran-C (Bidang Operasi), pp. 23-24.
36 Francisco interview.

as sergeants in the Indonesian army.[37]

*

During the 1975-77 period, Kopassandha demonstrated considerable flexibility as it tackled a range of strategic missions in the hills and jungles of East Timor. From massive deployments like Nanggala 8, to the comparatively tiny Nanggala 13, Indonesia's elite troops were at times called upon to demonstrate brute force, and other times required to exercise discretion and nuance. On one end of the scale, their gritty parachute assault at Suai had averted what they feared was an imminent visit by the Winspeare delegation.

On the other end of the scale, the creation of the Special Platoon showed great promise as a force multiplier. In mid-1976, this was highlighted to the top brass in Jakarta by Lieutenant Prabowo:

> During that early phase of the war, the generals to their credit wanted fast feedback from the frontlines. As a lowly first lieutenant, I was brought before the Operations Assistant to the Army Chief, Major General Alex Prawiraatmadja, and asked for my impressions. I knew about what *Pak* Hendro had done with the Special Platoon and told the general this was how to go forward: use indigenous troops, with Kopassandha giving advice and logistical support. Like what the Green Berets did with the Montagnards in Vietnam. I thought we could expand on the Special Platoon—maybe make a Special Battalion.
>
> They asked me to write a paper on this concept, and I did. But when they got around to making the first Timorese battalion a few years later, they decided to make it a conventional infantry battalion. And all of the cadre were Indonesian officers, not Timorese.[38]

For its part, Kopassandha remained at the forefront as Indonesia's counter-insurgency campaign in East Timor ebbed and flowed for another two decades. On more than a few occasions they would re-invented the wheel by raising new formations of Timorese partisans. This was done with varying degrees of success—and controversy.

But that's another tale for another time.

---

37 In April 1999, with an independence referendum looming, Belarmino ventured to Soibada in an attempt to recruit former Special Platoon members into a pro-Indonesia militia. After his efforts fell flat, Belarmino's vehicle was ambushed by Falintil guerrillas while driving back to Laklubar. An autopsy counted more than 70 bullet wounds on his body.

38 Prabowo interview.

INDEX

Alves, Leonardo da Costa 111-112, 113, 114n, 115, 120, 123
Amaral, Francisco Xavier do 16, 17, 26, 98, 101, 106, 122
Araujo, Arnaldo dos Reis 37, 97, 104
Ashuri 84

Badan Koordinasi Intelijen Negara, see Bakin
Bakin 16, 17, 37n
Belo, Tony 38, 39, 40, 52, 53, 87
Bertu, Felix 109, 118, 119, 123, 124, 125, 128

Central Intelligence Agency, 37n
Cruz, Belarmino Lopes da 109, 128
Cruz, Francisco Lopes da 97, 109

Dading Kalbuadi 24, 96, 107, 114, 116
Damung 48
Djasmin 69, 73
Dolfi Rondonuwu 48, 74, 90

Edo, see Hendropriyono, A.M.

Fathomi 49
Flamboyan (operation) 23, 116

Gatot Purwanto 116-117, 120, 122, 124
Gintings 74

Hendropriyono, A.M. 49, 93-96, 97, 99, 104, 107-108, 109, 110, 112, 113, 114, 115, 116-117, 118, 120, 121, 123, 124, 125, 126, 127
Heri Tabri 49

Jensen, Erik 33n-34n, 35, 37n, 52, 53, 81n, 87
Jonatas, Costa 17, 18n, 19n

Komodo (operation) 16-17, 21, 23, 81

Luhut Pandjaitan 91n
Lobato, Nicolau dos Reis 15-16, 17, 26, 40, 91, 102, 105-106, 118, 119, 121, 124

Malik, Adam 36, 51, 52, 81
Maman 91
Melati (operation) 25n
Moerdani, Leonardus Benjamin 23, 24, 69-70, 108
Moertopo, Ali 81
Moeryono, Johannes 43, 55, 76, 96, 126
Mota, Francisco 17, 18n, 19n

Muchdi Purwoprandjono 45, 46, 47, 49, 54, 55, 57, 59, 60, 71, 74, 76, 77, 84, 91, 126
Mulyadi 107

Nainggolan, Alberto 49, 72, 74, 82, 89, 91

Oliveira, Antonio Barbosa de 106, 110
Osorio Soares, Abilio 97, 98, 99, 103, 127
Osorio Soares, Domingos 98, 99
Osorio Soares, Elsa 103
Osorio Soares, Francisco 28n, 99, 100, 101, 102, 103, 104, 105, 106, 108,109, 110, 111, 112, 118, 120, 122, 125, 127, 128
Osorio Soares, Jose 15, 98, 101, 102, 104, 106
Osorio Soares, Lucia 98, 101
Osorio Soares, Manuel Vladimirio 98

Panggabean, Maraden 26
Peacock, Andrew 81
Prabowo Subianto 103,106, 127, 128

Ramahana, see Alves, Leonardo da Costa
Ramedi 72
Ramli Hasan Basri 107
Ramos-Horta, Jose 29-30, 35, 36, 37, 38, 51, 52, 53, 80, 81, 87
Rosendo 112, 113
Rudini 24
Rui Lopes 45, 89

Sanif, Muhammad 24, 44, 45, 56, 57, 60, 73, 75, 78
Santo, Domingos do Espirito 106, 112, 113, 125
Sarmento, Jose Maria 125
Sarmento, Vidal 105, 108, 109, 112n, 113, 118, 120, 125, 128
Schlitter-Silva, Gilberto 35
Simbolon, Eduardus 48
Sinaga, Johnny 57, 109, 113
Smaage, Harald 35
Soares, Abel 118
Soegito 25, 26, 73
Soekiman 43, 55, 57, 75, 76, 78, 82, 83, 84, 85, 86, 92, 96
Soeweno, Chamid 24
Sofyan Effendi 90n
Subagyo Hadi Siswoyo 49, 50, 58, 59, 71, 91, 93, 96n
Subagyo Saleh 69-70
Sudiman 54, 60, 76
Sudiyono 48, 90
Suharto 16, 20, 25, 36, 41, 46

Sukardjo 73
Sukarno 16, 50
Sunarpo 73
Suparmin 49, 58
Sutanto 43, 55
Sutedjo 69
Sutisna 58, 73
Suwarto 48
Suwito 59, 71, 74, 77, 86
Suyitno 76-77

Tarub 91n
Triyanto 85
Tukiman 84
Tukiran 123

U Thant 33, 34
Udin 73

Umpusinga, Hakim Saleh 48, 74, 90

Vietnam 17, 20

Wagimo 73
Wahid, Abdul 84
Waldheim, Kurt 30, 34, 81, 87
Warow Sende 43, 75
Wello, O.H. 69, 70
Winspeare, Vittorio 30, 31-37, 38, 39, 40, 51, 52, 53, 80, 81, 87
Wismoyo Arismunandar 69

Yogie Suardi Memet 41-42, 49, 55, 88, 97, 108, 115
Yunus Yosfiah 116

Zeka Vong 110, 113

www.ingramcontent.com/pod-product-compliance
Lightning Source LLC
Chambersburg PA
CBHW030942090426
42737CB00007B/512